Know Your Serger

Other books available from Chilton

Robbie Fanning, Series Editor

Contemporary Quilting Series

Fast Patch: A Treasury of Strip-Quilt Projects, by Anita Hallock

Fourteen Easy Baby Quilts, by Margaret Dittman

Machine-Quilted Jackets, Vests, and Coats, by Nancy Moore

Putting on the Glitz, by Anne Boyce and Sandra L. Hatch

The Quilter's Guide to Rotary Cutting, by Donna Poster

Scrap Quilts Using Fast Patch by Anita Hallock

Speed-Cut Quilts, by Donna Poster

Creative Machine Arts Series

The Button Lover's Book, by Marilyn Green

Claire Shaeffer's Fabric Sewing Guide

The Complete Book of Machine Embroidery, by Robbie and Tony Fanning

Creative Nurseries Illustrated, by Debra Terry and Juli Plooster

Creative Serging Illustrated, by Pati Palmer, Gail Brown, and Sue Green

Distinctive Serger Gifts and Crafts, by Naomi Baker and Tammy Young

The Expectant Mother's Wardrobe Planner, by Rebecca Dumlao

The Fabric Lover's Scrapbook, by Margaret Dittman

Friendship Quilts by Hand and Machine, by Carolyn Vosburg Hall

Innovative Sewing, by Gail Brown and Tammy Young

Innovative Serging, by Gail Brown and Tammy Young

Owner's Guide to Sewing Machines, Sergers, and Knitting Machines, by Gale Grigg Hazen

Petite Pizzazz, by Barb Griffin

Sew, Serge, Press, by Jan Saunders

Sewing and Collecting Vintage Fashions, by Eileen MacIntosh

Simply Serge Any Fabric, by Naomi Baker and Tammy Young

Twenty Easy Machine-Made Rugs, by Jackie Dodson

Know Your Sewing Machine Series, by Jackie Dodson

Know Your Bernina, second edition

Know Your Brother, with Jane Warnick

Know Your Elna, with Carol Ahles

Know Your New Home, with Judi Cull and Vicki Lyn Hastings

Know Your Pfaff, with Audrey Griese

Know Your Sewing Machine

Know Your Singer

Know Your Viking, with Jan Saunders

Know Your Serger Series, by Tammy Young and Naomi Baker

Know Your baby lock

Know Your Pfaff Hobbylock

Know Your White Superlock

Teach Yourself to Sew Better Series, by Jan Saunders

A Step-by-Step Guide to Your Bernina

A Step-by-Step Guide to Your New Home

A Step-by-Step Guide to Your Sewing Machine

A Step-by-Step Guide to Your Viking

Know Your Serger

Naomi Baker and Tammy Young

Chilton Book Company

Radnor, Pennsylvania

Published in Radnor, Pennsylvania 19089, by Chilton Book Company

Cover Design by Tony Jacobson
Designed by Martha Vercoutere
Illustrations by Chris Hansen

Manufactured in the United States of America

Library of Congress Cataloging in Publication Data

Baker, Naomi
  Know your Serger / Naomi Baker and Tammy Young.

      p. cm.—(Creative machine arts)
  Includes bibliographical references and index.
  1. Serging 2. Sewing machines.
  I. Young, Tammy. II. Title.
  III. Series: Creative machine arts series.
TT713.B33247 1992   91-58291
646.2'044—dc20   CIP
ISBN 0-8019-8241-3 (pb)

1 2 3 4 5 6 7 8 9 0 1 0 9 8 7 6 5 4 3 2

Contents

Preface

The fun continues! After writing three brand-specific decorative serging books in the last two years (*Know Your baby lock, Know Your White Superlock,* and *Know Your Pfaff Hobbylock*), we have been asked repeatedly for a similar book applying to all brands. And here it is.

Serger techniques and technology have advanced rapidly over the past decade, and enthusiasts have taken serger sewing from a few basic stitches to a wide variety of decorative applications and innovative uses. We call the latest developments in decorative serger sewing **ornamental serging.**

In this book, you'll learn some of the same ornamental serging techniques presented in the first three books **plus** lots of **new information and all new projects.** Special sections on heirloom serging, weaving serged strips, and thread-chain jewelry have been included.

All the serger companies have regularly upgraded their serger models, adding features and accessories to make ornamental serging techniques easier to master. But no matter what your serger brand or model, what feet or attachments you own, or how old your machine is, any basic 3-thread serger stitch can be used to create a variety of exciting decorative effects.

Know Your Serger is our latest book in a series designed to encourage you to take your serger beyond the basics and develop its potential as an artistic instrument. In it we outline methods for seaming, edge-finishing, binding and trimming, embellishing fabric, serger chain art, and other decorative serging techniques. Simple projects at the end of each lesson allow you to easily practice the skills taught.

So breeze through the basics (if you haven't already), and begin exploring the wide variety of options for serging one-of-a-kind creations.

Happy ornamental serging,

Naomi Baker and Tammy Young

Foreword

Those of us lucky enough to own a serger need no convincing that as an invention, it ranks right up there with Post-it Notes, rotary cutters, and the microwave.

Yet those of us brave enough to tell the whole truth will confess that we've barely scratched the surface of our serger's capabilities.

I'm no different. Though I'm devoted to my serger, I've used it primarily to clean finish seam allowances. I'd like to do more, but my time for experimenting is limited. What I need is a master teacher at my side, coaxing me to twirl those knobs, change that thread, try this technique.

Shazam! Not one, but two master teachers have appeared through a puff of smoke. Tammy and Naomi, in the pages of this book, are exactly what you and I need. They walk us through the basics, and then lesson by lesson, teach a new technique, ending with a sample project using that technique. Some of my favorite ornamental serging techniques are the serged frog closure, elastic button loops, and double-bound seams.

For a busy sewer, this lesson format is ideal. You can try a lesson in an evening, make a sample for your notebook, then choose your favorite techniques to embellish a garment on the weekend.

By the time you finish, you will truly know your serger.

Robbie Fanning
Series Editor

Acknowledgments

We again want to thank two very hard-working, talented people without whom our books would not be completed. Chris Hansen is one of those rare individuals who both sews and draws beautifully. His illustrations bring our techniques and project ideas to life. Martha Vercoutere, who does our book design and preparation, is another gem. Her attention to detail and her ability to work under a deadline are much appreciated.

In addition, many thanks to editorial assistant Cate Keller. Her skill and diligence have helped us so much during the final preparation stages of all our books. And our sincere appreciation to Cherene Holland, our very capable manuscript editor.

Thanks also to the industry professionals who have pioneered serger sewing and continually inspire us. And a special thanks to our friend Gail Brown, who originated several of the techniques presented in this book.

Finally, many thanks go to our editor, Robbie Fanning, and our publisher's representative, Kathryn Conover, for believing in our efforts and encouraging us to write a series of books on ornamental serging techniques.

The following are registered trademark names used in this book: *Decor 6, Fabric Mender Magic, Fray Check, Friendly Plastic, Lycra, OK to Wash-It, Perfect Pleater, Rainbow Elastic Plus, Seams Great, Solvy, Ultraleather, Ultrasuede, Velcro, Wash-Away,* and *Wonder-Under.*

1. Serger Basics

- **Begin the Adventure**
- **Serging and Sewing Strategies**
- **How to Use This Book**
- **Serger Stitch Formation**
- **Optional Features and Accessories**
- **Loving Care**
- **Basic Troubleshooting**

Begin the Adventure

Why did *you* decide to buy a serger? For many of us, a demonstration of its creative potential was the clincher. Not only could it seam and finish allowances quickly and neatly, it also could be used for rolled edges, flatlocking, and a variety of additional decorative stitches and techniques. (Fig. 1-1)

But when we arrived home with the new machine, doubts may have started to surface. For many, the biggest hurdle to overcome in the exciting adventure of serger sewing is **taking the machine out of the box.** Yes, that's right! Over the years, we've found that for many home-sewers, the serger looked wonderful when demonstrated in the store, but at home it seemed daunting and compli-

Fig. 1-1: *The serger's creative potential makes it an appealing purchase.*

cated. (After all, it's an entirely different kind of machine than the sewing machine we all have known.) So into the closet it goes, just waiting for that rainy day when there's plenty of time to figure out how to use it and to practice all of those wonderful serger techniques.

Of course, the longer the serger stays in the closet, the more complex and intimidating it seems. Meanwhile, your "friendly" sewing machine is right there to fall back on.

The next hurdle in serger use occurs when we do take the machine out of the box, and the dealer has adjusted it for perfectly balanced stitching. We can serge beautiful seams and edges, but heaven forbid that we might have to switch to a rolled edge or a flatlock. Horrors! That can involve taking out a needle, changing a foot, and adjusting the tension settings. The thought of tackling all these separate steps seems overwhelming at first.

But just stop and consider how many different adjustments you make effortlessly on your sewing machine—winding the bobbin, threading, changing needles and feet, making stitch-length adjustments, and converting to special stitches. The serger only seems complicated at first, when we're getting used to it and to its unique method of sewing.

There's a simple answer. Take your serger out of the box, read the owner's instruction manual, and practice the various kinds of stitches available on your model. In other words, **use your serger and you'll become comfortable with it sooner than you think.**

Serger expert Sue Green-Baker calls this process "bonding." Although the term is most often used for parents'

feelings toward their child or for other personal relationships, it applies nicely to serger sewing as well. As you spend more time with your machine and get to know it, you will learn its idiosyncrasies, talents, and personality. At varying times this bonding process can be frustrating, exciting, intimidating, or rewarding—and just plain fun. Sharpening your spirit of adventure can be a big help.

If serging classes are available to you, by all means take advantage of them. They're a great way to speed up the learning process, pick up tips and techniques, and have a good time in the process.

In this book, we assume that you have already learned the basics of serger sewing. Check the following list to be sure:

—— Threading
—— Changing and balancing tension
—— Changing stitch width and length
—— Adjusting for a rolled edge. (Practice until you can do it effortlessly.)
—— Adjusting for flatlocking
—— Using the differential feed
—— Changing needles
—— Cleaning your machine—and oiling it
—— Clearing the stitch finger
—— Serging inside and outside corners
—— Ripping out stitches

Your owner's manual is a must. If you don't have one, buy or order one from your dealer. The manual contains detailed instructions on the basics listed above. Work your way through the

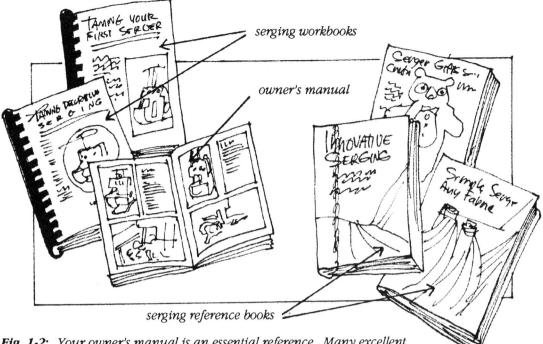

Fig. 1-2: *Your owner's manual is an essential reference. Many excellent serging books and workbooks are also available.*

manual early in your bonding process. (Fig. 1-2)

In addition to your manual, extensive information is available to lead you through all the machine basics and construction techniques and beyond. (Several excellent resources are listed under Other Books by the Authors, including the comprehensive beginner's book, *ABCs of Serging.*)

When sergers were first introduced in the United States, their use was limited to simple seams and edge-finishes. Since then, serger sewing enthusiasts have developed a great deal of information and many exciting new techniques. As you get to know your serger and put it to work, you will discover a whole new world of ornamental serging possibilities.

Serging and Sewing Strategies

Your serger is a natural companion to your sewing machine. Rather than working in competition with each other, these two machines team up to offer us endless possibilities. Once you are familiar with your serger and all its potential uses, you will soon know when to use your sewing machine and when to use your serger for any project or parts of a project.

The serger is fast, finishes edges beautifully, makes neat, sturdy seams, and replicates many of the looks found in today's couture and ready-to-wear. It efficiently sews many specialty fabrics we would have hesitated to tackle in the past, including sheers, silkies, and loosely wovens. The built-in stretch of a serger stitch also makes serging a favored option for interlocks, *Lycra* blends, and sweatering.

We've often heard that the serger speeds up sewing, that it trims, seams, and overlocks in one step, that it makes beautiful rolled edges and has many decorative uses. But the one thing we don't always hear is that **serger sewing is all about edges.**

Because the loopers must go above and below the fabric in order to form an overlock stitch, most serging must necessarily be done on edges or folds. (Fig. 1-3) The one exception is a double chainstitch formed by the needle and a looper (not available on all serger models).

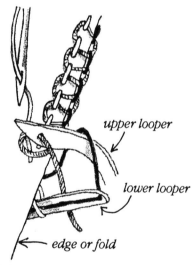

upper looper

lower looper

edge or fold

Fig. 1-3: *Because of a serger's looper mechanism, always place serging on an edge or fold.*

The serger's ability to sew on edges includes seams (see Chapter 3), flatlocking (in Lessons 3 and 25), and edge-finishing (discussed in Chapter 4). Beyond these basics, interesting variations abound.

The sewing machine, unlike the serger, has the ability to sew anywhere on a piece of fabric, not just on an edge or fold. Its straight-stitch capability—for top-stitching and edge-stitching—is essential to supplement many serger techniques. Also, the sewing machine's decorative stitches can be combined with serging to enhance your creativity.

Plan each of your sewing projects (whether garments, accessories, or home decorating items) in advance. Where can you add ornamental details for the most artistic and pleasing results? Consider possibilities for seams and edges. Consider decorative flatlocking. What are your other options? (Fig. 1-4)

Fig. 1-4: *Plan your serging projects with decorative detail in mind.*

Experiment, then give it your best shot. But remember, subtlety can often be more pleasing than overdoing it, so you needn't decorate every edge or seam on any one project. Choose those areas where your ornamental serging will be the most effective.

The lessons and projects throughout this book are just a beginning. Once you understand the basics of serger sewing, you too can become a serger artist. It's simply a matter of focus and awareness.

Practice, experimentation, failure, and success are all part of the process. So accept the challenge and join us in the latest phase of serger sewing—ornamental serging.

How to Use This Book

Know Your Serger has been designed to lead you quickly through the basics (Chapters 1 and 2) and into the fun world of ornamental serging. You'll find 38 lessons, grouped into chapters on seams; edges; trims, braids, and bindings; special techniques; fabric embellishment; and chain-art possibilities.

The lessons begin with decorative basics and progress to those requiring more advanced skill. We include a simple project at the end of every lesson so you can easily practice the techniques you have learned.

Less experienced serger users may want to follow the lessons numerically to learn basic skills before moving on to advanced ones. If you come to a term you don't understand, refer to the Glossary of Serging Terms. Experienced seamsters can easily skip around in the book, choosing to study a lesson when it applies to a current project.

Regardless of your level of experience, the Table of Contents can help you decide quickly which decorative seams, edges, bindings, or other techniques to use for a particular serger project. Once you've mastered all of the lessons in *Know Your Serger*, you'll feel comfortable selecting even the most advanced ornamental serging applications.

Serger Stitch Formation

Every serger model will produce at least one stitch type. Most models have one or more optional stitches, and some (especially 4- and 5-thread models) can serge many different stitches. Refer to your owner's manual to determine the stitches available on your machine. If this book is your own, use a highlighter pen to mark your model's features.

2-Thread Overedge Stitch
(Fig. 1-5)

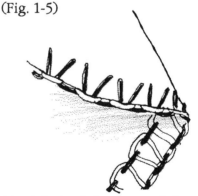

Fig. 1-5: *Stitch formation—2-thread overedge.*

- Less bulky than 3- or 4-thread stitching.

- Threads do not lock at the seamline, so this stitch is not used for basic seaming.

- Used for lightweight edge-finishing, flatlocking, or flatlock seaming.

2-Thread Double Chainstitch
(Fig. 1-6)

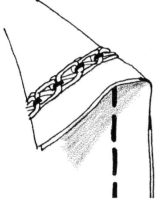

Fig. 1-6: Stitch formation—2-thread double chainstitch.

- The left needle forms a straight stitch on top of the fabric, and a looper thread interlocks to form a chain on the underside.

- A locking stitch with little or no stretch.

- Used for top-stitching, seaming, or hemming. When top-stitching or hemming from the underside (with the chain on the right side), a more pronounced stitching line is visible.

3-Thread Overlock Stitch
(Fig. 1-7)

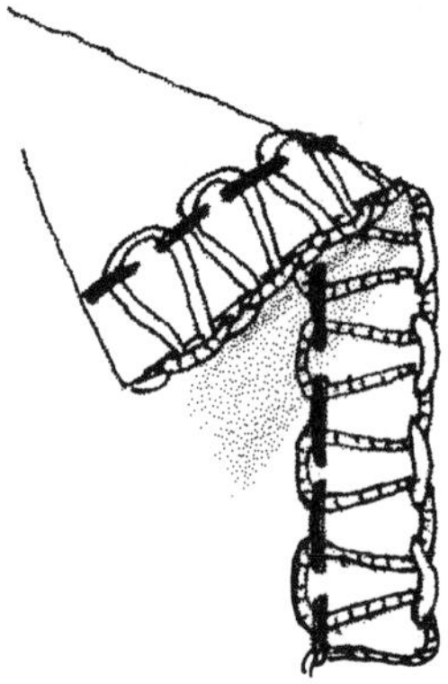

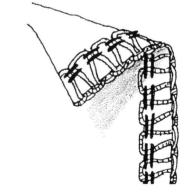

Fig. 1-7: Stitch formation—3-thread overlock.

- Threads interlock at the seamline to form a stretchable, yet durable, seam or edge-finish.

- Available on practically all serger models.

- Less bulky than a 4- or 5-thread stitch.

3/4-Thread Overlock Stitch
(Fig. 1-8)

Fig. 1-8: Stitch formation—3/4-thread overlock.

- Sometimes called a 4-thread overlock or overedge stitch.

- Formed with two looper threads and two needle threads.

- The upper and lower looper threads interlock with both the right and left needle threads.

- Durable for seaming and decorative finishing (up to 7.5mm wide) and fully stretchable.

- Converts to a 3-thread overlock stitch by removing either needle. Use the left needle for a wide stitch and the right needle for a narrower stitch.

4-Thread Mock Safety Stitch

(Fig. 1-9)

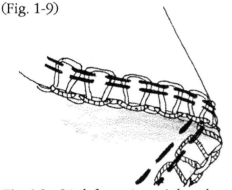

Fig. 1-9: Stitch formation—4-thread mock safety stitch.

- Sometimes referred to as a variation of the 3/4-thread overlock stitch (they're never both available on the same machine).

- The upper looper interlocks with the right needle thread (but not the left) on top of the fabric.

- Converts to a narrow, 3-thread overlock or 2-thread overedge stitch by removing the left needle. Will not form a wide, 2- or 3-thread stitch with the left needle.

- Durable and stretchable for seaming and decorative finishing.

4-Thread Safety Stitch

(Fig. 1-10)

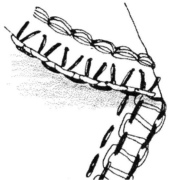

Fig. 1-10: Stitch formation—4-thread safety stitch.

- Often called a 4/2-thread stitch.

- A combination of a double chainstitch and a 2-thread overedge stitch. Essentially, a chainstitched seam with a finished edge.

- The stitch can be converted to the chain only or to the overedge only.

- A nonstretch stitch used for loosely woven fabrics and to stabilize stretchy areas.

5-Thread Safety Stitch

(Fig. 1-11)

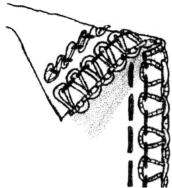

Fig. 1-11: *Stitch formation—5-thread safety stitch.*

■ Combination of a double chainstitch (on the seamline) and a 3-thread overlock stitch (on the edge).

■ Stitch width up to 9mm wide.

■ Can be converted to a double chainstitch only or a 3-thread overlock only. Some models can also convert to a 4-thread stitch and a 2-thread overedge.

■ The most stable seam and finish, used most often on loosely wovens and for stabilizing stretchy areas.

Optional Features and Accessories

Some serger models have advanced, built-in features to help make ornamental serging easier. Some also have special feet and attachments for specific decorative-serging applications. No model has every option. Look for these helpful features and decide which are most important for your individual serging needs:

■ **Easy threading**—many manufacturers have designed features such as a self-threading lower looper, a built-in needle threader, easily accessible thread guides (the cover swings out to completely expose the loopers), a swing-out presser foot, and a color-coded threading system to speed up the threading process. Because you will change thread often in decorative serging, these features can be very helpful.

■ **Easy adjustments**—it's faster and more convenient to be able to make as many adjustments as possible (stitch width, stitch length, and differential feed) from the outside of the machine while you're serging. Also look for a simple rolled-edge conversion; on some newer models, you'll simply move or remove the stitch finger and won't need to change the foot or needle plate or both. (Fig. 1-12)

■ **Differential feed**—although successful decorative serging is possible without it, this feature makes control of the fabric much simpler. The machine's two sets of feed dogs can be adjusted to control how taut or compacted the fabric is as it's being serged over. Differential feed can prevent puckering on lightweight or sheer fabrics and stretching of knits or loosely wovens, plus it can be used for easing or gathering.

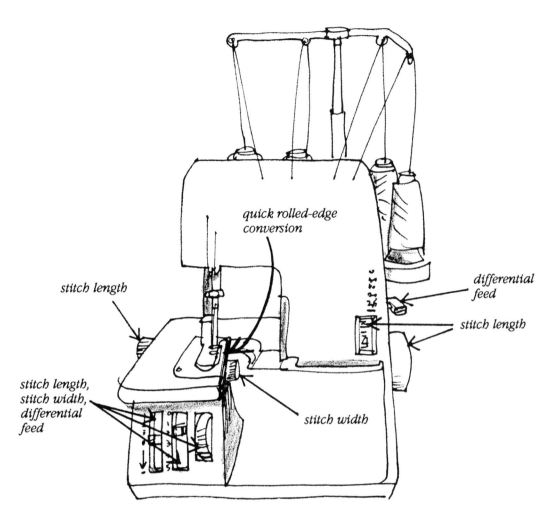

Fig. 1-12: *Look for easy adjustments to speed up ornamental serging.*

■ **Wide-width stitches**—when featuring serging as a decorative element on a garment or project, we often use the widest possible stitch for the most dramatic effect. Currently, a 9mm 5-thread safety stitch is the widest available. The widest possible 3- or 3/4-thread stitch is 7.5mm.

■ **Cording guides**—some models have guides on the machine or the standard presser foot to feed heavy thread or cording so it can be serged over accurately. On some models, the guide is wide enough to accommodate elastic or tape as well. This is another appealing

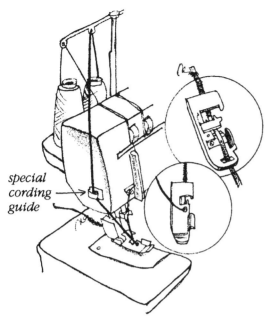

special
cording
guide

Fig. 1-13: *Cord guides on the machine and/or presser foot position cording, narrow ribbon, or tape while serging over it.*

feature for decorative serging techniques. (Fig. 1-13)

■ **Tension release**—on a few models only, this handy lever releases the tension on all the threads. It's used for quick thread changes, for easily removing work from under the presser foot without chaining off, and for simple securing of the stitching when beginning and ending a seam.

■ **Computerized stitch guide**—some newer sergers have a liquid-crystal, computerized display (LCD). The panel indicates the tension, stitch length, differential feed setting, and other settings necessary for the stitch you've selected. Then you make the adjustments.

■ **Disengageable knife**—for some decorative-serging techniques, you'll want to avoid cutting the edge (when serging over a fold, elastic, or previous stitching, for example). On some models, one of the two knives can be raised or lowered to prevent any mishaps. (Fig. 1-14)

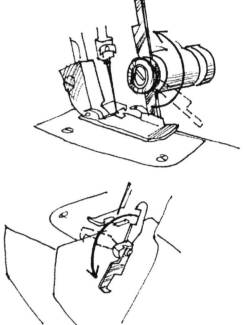

Fig. 1-14: *To prevent decorative-serging mishaps, some machines have a disengageable knife.*

■ **Two-speed foot control**—several new serger models have an electronic foot control with both half-speed and full-speed positions. The slower half-speed setting allows greater control in ornamental serging, especially when using heavier decorative thread.

■ **Snap-on feet**—presser feet often have a snap-on feature so you can change easily from one foot to another. They also provide unrestricted access when

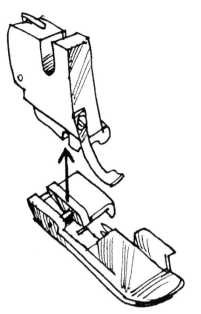

Fig. 1-15: *Snap-on feet are available on some serger models.*

threading and changing needles. (Fig. 1-15)

■ **Optional presser feet**—most serger models have one or more optional feet for specialized serging techniques. Ask your dealer which feet are available for your machine. (Fig. 1-16)

Blindhem foot—this handy optional foot can be used for serged tucks and for accurately guiding serger stitching along a fold, as well as for blindhemming. For specific uses, see perfecting flatlocking (Lessons 3 and 25) and serger lace (Lesson 24).

Elastic foot—used to easily guide and stretch narrow elastic during application. The foot can be adjusted to vary the stretch of the elastic as it is being serged over. See elasticized trims (Lesson 18) and serge-shirring (Lesson 23) for applications.

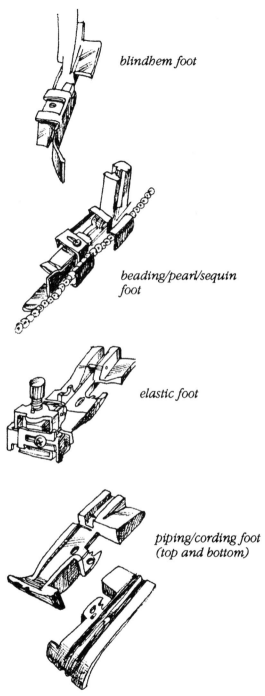

blindhem foot

beading/pearl/sequin foot

elastic foot

piping/cording foot (top and bottom)

Fig. 1-16: *Some of these optional presser feet are available for most sergers.*

Beading/pearl/sequin foot—this foot guides pearls and beads between the needle and the knives so they can be serged over. It can also be used when serging over wire (Lessons 7 and 24) and for serging over trim (Lesson 27) or cording (Lesson 4).

Ribbon/tape foot—available for some models that don't feature a cording or tape guide in the standard foot, this optional foot is designed to guide ribbon, tape, or cording when serging over it. (See Fig. 4-5) Especially applicable for serging over trim (Lesson 27), this foot also works well for serge-cording (Lesson 4).

Piping/cording foot—although this foot looks similar to a standard presser foot, it has a groove in the bottom to accommodate piping. It's used to make and apply serged piping (Lesson 14) or for a double rolled edge (Lessons 5 and 17).

■ **Novelty accessories**—some serger models feature other specialized accessories such as a bias binder (used with a 2-thread double chainstitch to fold, position, and attach a binding strip), a fabric separator (used with differential feed to gather one layer as it's serge-seamed to another), a tape guide (to fold and position a tape strip for a piping-like seam insertion), stitching guides (to position fabric accurately as it is serged), or a free arm (to help reach difficult areas).

Loving Care

Your serger is a precision instrument. If you treat it well, it will reward you with years of ornamental serging. But without proper care, it can create problems on even the simplest project.

You may not be taking your sewing machine in for regular checkups, but for your serger regular checkups are essential. The serger's timing and accuracy need to be much more finely tuned than the sewing machine's.

Follow these basic guidelines to keep your serger running smoothly: (Fig. 1-17)

After Every Project

____ Remove the presser foot, needle plate, and needle(s).

____ Remove **large pieces of lint** with a fluffed-out lint brush.

____ Blow out **fine lint** with environmentally-safe pressurized air, a hair dryer, a computer vacuum, or a household vacuum on reversed air flow. OR...

____ Use a lint brush lightly dipped in sewing machine oil to remove **fine lint** particles. The oil also provides some gentle lubrication.

 Note: Never blow into your serger to remove lint particles. The small amount of moisture in your breath can harm your machine.

At least every third project

____ Change the needle(s).

■ Use the correct type and size of needle for your fabric.

■ Push the needle(s) all the way up into the needle bar.

■ Be sure the long groove is centered at the front of the needle.

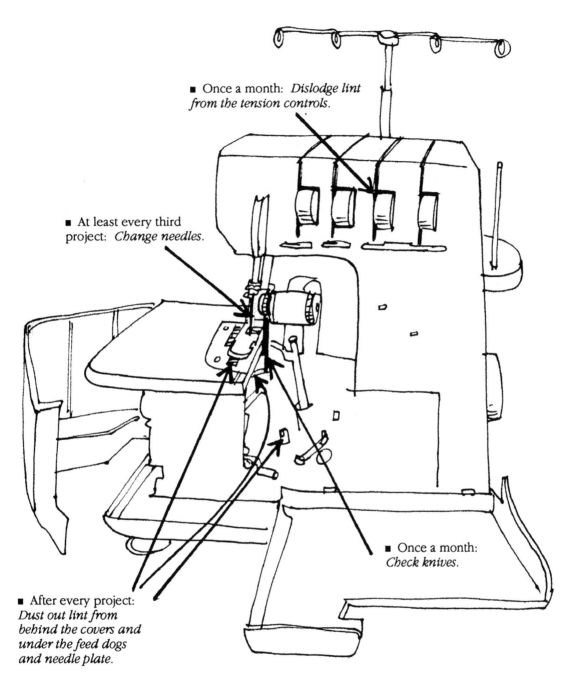

■ Once a month: *Dislodge lint from the tension controls.*

■ At least every third project: *Change needles.*

■ Once a month: *Check knives.*

■ After every project: *Dust out lint from behind the covers and under the feed dogs and needle plate.*

Fig. 1-17: *Follow these basic guidelines to keep your serger running smoothly.*
■ At least every 12-15 serging hours: *Oil only if your model requires it.*
■ Once a year: *Take your serger to your local dealer for a checkup.*

At least every 12 to 15 hours of serging

N **Note:** Oil your serger, if it requires oiling at all (some models do not; see your manual). Use only sewing machine oil.

_____ If your serger is noisier than usual, oil it.

_____ If you haven't used your serger for several months, oil it before using it again.

_____ After oiling, test-serge on scraps of fabric to remove any residual oil.

Once a Month

_____ Remove lint lodged in the tension controls.

■ Turn the tension controls to zero.

■ Put knotted thread through the tension discs.

■ Reset the tensions to normal and pull the knotted thread back and forth through the discs to remove any lint.

_____ Check the knives.

■ Do they cut ragged edges?

■ Do they have a shiny, worn look?

■ If so, replace one or both knives (refer to your manual for instructions or see your local dealer).

Once a Year

_____ Take your serger to your local dealer for an annual checkup.

_____ Stock up on needles, new accessories, and the latest books and information.

Basic Troubleshooting

Problem	Cause
Thread Breaks	Incorrectly threaded Tension too tight Thread caught on thread stand, thread guide, or spool Poor-quality thread Needle incorrect size or bent Needle inserted incorrectly
Needle Breaks	Needle bent or damaged Needle not fully inserted Fabric pulled while serging

Skipped or Irregular Stitches	Needle bent or damaged
	Needle not fully inserted
	Incorrect needle
	Incorrectly threaded
	Tension too tight
	Telescoping stand not fully extended
	Thread caught on thread stand,
	    thread guide, or spool
	Thread not securely engaged
	    in tension discs
	Skipped thread guide

Puckered Seams	Needle tension too tight Differential feed on low setting Thread caught on thread stand, thread guide, or spool
Ragged Cutting	Dull knife Nicks in knife Incorrect placement of knife
Fabric Doesn't Feed	Knife disengaged Dull knife Presser foot up

2. Ornamental Serging Basics

- **Tension—The Key to Success**
- **Decorative Threads**
- **Troubleshooting with Decorative Thread**
- **Threads Other Than Decorative**
- **Shaping Materials**
- **Other Important Serging Supplies**
- **Ornamental Serging Sample Book**
- **Exploring Your Machine's Creative Limits**

Tension—The Key to Success

Once you have a thorough knowledge of serger tension adjustment, you will be able to use your machine to its fullest creative potential. On your sewing machine, you would change the tension only if there were something wrong with the stitch. *On a serger, you will readjust your tension settings often because of differences in thread, fabric, or stitch type.* You will also change tensions as you change the stitch length and width and when you want to create varied effects.

Although tension adjustment is part of any basic serger instruction, we will cover it again because it is such a critical part of ornamental serging.

Changing serger tension settings is not complicated if you follow a few basic guidelines and know what a correctly adjusted stitch should look like. In a balanced 3-thread overlock stitch, the looper threads should hug the top and bottom of the fabric and overlock exactly

on the edge. The needle thread should form a line along the left edge of the stitch and look like sewing machine straight-stitching on both top and bottom. (Fig. 2-1)

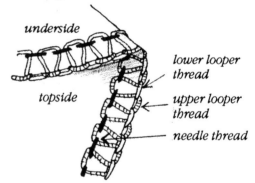

Fig. 2-1: *When tension settings are balanced, the looper threads will hug the top and bottom of the fabric and overlock exactly on the cut edge.*

See your owner's manual or refer to Chapter 1 for examples of perfectly balanced tension for all the stitch options on your serger.

Practicing tension adjustment

If you have never experimented with your machine's tension settings, or if you have any doubt about how to adjust the serger tension properly, try this experiment:

1. Thread your serger with different colors of all-purpose or serger thread. (For easier identification, you may want to use the same colors as those on your thread guides.) If you have a 4- or 5-thread machine, adjust for a 3-thread overlock stitch and test that first. Later you can convert to other stitch configurations and test them as well. Adjust for a medium-length (3mm), balanced stitch.

2. Find the center of all your settings. Try to set the control as close to the middle setting as possible. If you tend to forget which control adjusts which looper or needle, label them with small pieces of masking tape. Study your manual and place each label on the correct control until you know it by heart. (Some models are labeled for you.)

3. Set the lower looper tension on its lowest (loosest) setting. Leave the upper looper and needle tension on the middle setting.

4. Cut two 4" by 6" rectangles from mediumweight woven fabric. Serge-seam the rectangles together along one side and examine the results. Learn what the lower looper thread looks like when the tension is at its lowest setting. Label and save your seam sample for your sample book (see page 29).

5. Set your lower looper tension almost all the way (but not quite) to the highest (tightest) setting. Leave the upper looper and needle tensions at the middle settings. Repeat step 4, checking the results of a tightened lower looper tension. Label and save your sample.

6. Turn the lower looper tension back to the middle setting and loosen the upper looper tension all the way. Leave the lower looper and needle tension on the middle settings. Repeat step 4, checking the results of a loosened upper looper tension. Label and save your sample.

7. Repeat step 5 for the upper looper by tightening the tension and leaving the lower looper and needle tensions on the middle settings.

Balancing the tension

Now you are beginning to understand the effects of changing the tension settings on your serger—and you're no longer afraid to experiment! The next step is to learn how to adjust for a balanced tension:

1. Set the tension controls at their middle settings.

2. Cut long 4"-wide strips from medium-weight woven fabric for testing. Put the right sides of two long strips together and serge a test seam for a few inches on the long edge.

3. Stop and look at the stitching behind the presser foot without removing the fabric. Look at the upper and lower looper threads. Remember, the looper threads should meet at the edge. If one thread is pulled *over* the edge, the other thread is too tight. First, find the one that appears to be too tight and **loosen** it.

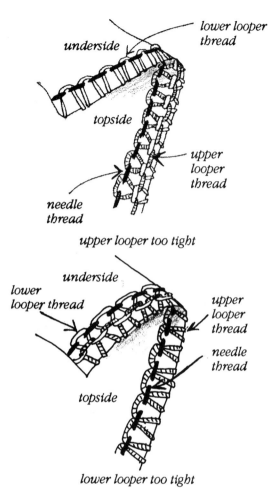

upper looper too tight

lower looper too tight

Fig. 2-2: *Find the looper tension that is too tight and loosen it.*

(Fig. 2-2) Serge a few more inches. If the tension hasn't been eased or has been tightened further, return the control to the original position and **tighten** the other looper thread (the one that appears to be too loose). Continue to test-serge and adjust—a few inches at a time—until the looper tensions are balanced.

4. Examine the needle-thread line from the right side. If it is too loose, the seamline will pull open. If it is too tight,

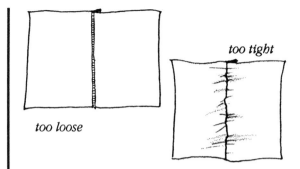

too loose

too tight

Fig. 2-3: *When the needle tension is too loose, the seamline will pull open. When the needle tension is too tight, the seamline will pucker.*

the seamline will pucker. (Fig. 2-3) The needle-thread tension won't always need to be adjusted. Change the needle tension only if the seamline pulls open or looks puckered. Turn the tension control to a higher number to tighten or to a lower number to loosen.

Follow these guidelines to get perfectly balanced tension every time:

1. Adjust one control at a time and test-serge after each adjustment. Don't make the mistake of turning all the tension controls at the same time.

2. Make only small adjustments. A small adjustment can make a big difference.

3. When adjusting the looper tension, first loosen the looper thread that appears to be too tight. If the adjustment doesn't seem to help the problem, or if it makes it worse, **turn the control back to where it was** and tighten the other looper tension. Continue adjusting, one control at a time (setting the control back to where you started if the change did not help), until you have balanced the tension.

4. Every time you use a different type of thread or fabric, you will need to check your tension adjustments. For the most accurate adjustments, test-serge on scraps of the actual project fabric, using the same grain and the same number of layers.

Continue to practice, test, and experiment with varying fabrics and tensions. Learn to recognize what happens when you make tension adjustments. As you proceed through this book, you will find that *some very interesting novelty stitches can be formed by varying the tensions.* Both the rolled-edge stitch and flatlocking are created with tension adjustments. And that's only the beginning of a wide range of possibilities.

Confidence in using your serger and the ability to use it to its full potential come only after you are comfortable with changing tensions.

Decorative Threads

We're constantly learning about new or newly discovered threads, yarns, ribbons, and trims that can be serged ornamentally. Creative serger enthusiasts have used everything from elastic thread to fine wire to create special ornamental effects.

Many materials for decorative serging can be found in the notions and trim departments of your local fabric store. Also try sewing machine dealerships; needlecraft, yarn, and craft shops; and mail-order sources.

Follow the thread selection guidelines in the Decorative Serging Quick Reference Chart on pages 20-21 as a starting point for ornamental serging possibilities.

Special Tip: The easiest threads to use are decorative threads crosswound on top-feeding cones. (Fig. 2-4) Those wound in balls or skeins or sold by the yard are more difficult because they require extra care in helping them feed evenly when serging.

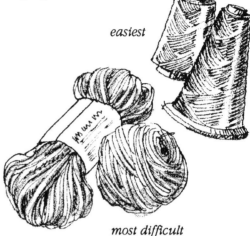

easiest

most difficult

Fig. 2-4: Crosswound decorative thread is easiest to use. Balls and skeins are more difficult.

Because not all decorative threads will serge successfully in every machine, always test first. Allow at least seven yards for each looper you'll be testing and two yards for each needle. When estimating actual project yardage required, you will need ten times the finished decorative serging length for each looper.

Serging with decorative thread

You have three options when serging with decorative thread: threading it through the loopers, threading it through the needle, or serging over it.

Decorative Serging Quick Reference Chart

Use: N - Needle
    UL - Upper Looper
    LL - Lower Looper
    SO - Serge Over
    A - All Uses

EASE:
  * Easy
  ** Moderate
  *** Challenging

Tension Adjustment: N - None
    S - Slight
    L - Lots

TYPE	SIZES AND COLORS AVAILABLE	USE	EASE OF USE	TENSION ADJUST-MENT	SUBSTI-TUTE	DESCRIPTION	APPLICATION	NOTES
Buttonhole Twist	Variety of colors.	A	*	N-S		Slightly heavier than all-purpose thread.	Edging or flatlock seaming all types sportswear, home decorator items.	May work satisfactorily in size 14 needle, not in size 11.
Woolly Nylon	Variety, including variegated and metallic	A	*	S		Crimped, yarn-like thread, stretchy, fluffs up when serged. May melt with hot iron.	Excellent for rolled edge, other decorative edges, and flatlocking. Soft elastic seams on lingerie, swimwear, activewear.	May be used through needle. Tensions may need to be adjusted. Best coverage of any lightweight decorative thread.
Rayon	Variety of colors and sizes, including new "pearl" rayon.	A	*	N-S-L (depend-ing on size)		Shiny, silk-like thread, smooth, bright colors.	High-luster edging or flatlock seaming for elegant fashion garments and accessories.	
Silk	Variety of colors and sizes.	A	*	N-S	Rayon Threads, Machine Embroidery	Shiny, soft, smooth, expensive.	High-luster edging or flatlock seaming for elegant fashion garments and accessories.	
Metallics	Variety of sizes and colors, including variegated.	A	**	S-L		Adds glitter, can be used multi-strand or combined with other threads.	Highly decorative edge for sportswear, eveningwear, holiday gifts, and home decor.	Vary greatly according to manufacturer. Avoid those with coarse, metal fibers. Experiment to find which works best.
Braids	Variety of sizes, colors and fibers.	UL, LL, SO	** to ***	L		Purchase by the yard.	Edging or flatlocking of garments, accessories, home decorator, and nursery items.	Require testing and experiments to achieve tension balance. It may be necessary to bypass tension disc altogether. Use in loopers only.

Decorative Serging Quick Reference Chart

Type	Description	Code	Symbol	L/N/S		Characteristics	Uses	Notes
Ribbon	Variety of colors, fibers, including silk, acrylic, polyester. 1/16 – 1/4" wide.	UL, LL SO	***	L	Braided Rayon Ribbon	Soft knitting ribbon, bright colors.	Edging or flatlocking of garments, accessories, home decorator, and nursery items.	Require testing and experimentation to achieve tension balance. It may be necessary to bypass tension disc altogether. Use in loopers only.
Braided Rayon Ribbon (Ribbon Floss)	Variety of colors, including metallic. 1/8" wide.	UL, LL SO	**	L		Soft knitting ribbon, bright colors crosswound on tube.	Edging or flatlocking of garments, accessories, home decorator, and nursery items.	Require testing and experimentation to achieve tension balance. It may be necessary to bypass tension disc altogether. Use in loopers only.
Crochet Thread	Variety of colors, including variegated and metallic.	UL, LL SO	** to ***	L		Available in acrylic and cotton, strong thread.	Edging or flatlocking of garments, accessories, home decorator, and nursery items.	Require testing and experimentation to achieve tension balance. It may be necessary to bypass tension disc altogether. Use in loopers only.
Pearl Cotton	Variety of colors and sizes—#5 and 8 are most common.	UL, LL SO	#8 ** / #5 ***	L	Crochet thread, Rayon "pearl"	Soft, shiny, tightly twisted, strong thread.	Edging or flatlocking of garments, accessories, home decorator, and nursery items.	Require testing and experimentation to achieve tension balance. It may be necessary to bypass tension disc altogether. Use in loopers only.
Yarns	Variety of colors. Two- or three-ply. Baby or Sport yarn.	UL, LL SO	*** (Two-ply easiest)	L	Pearl cotton, Woolly nylon	Soft, smooth, tightly twisted.	Edging or flatlocking of garments, accessories, home decorator, and nursery items.	Require testing and experimentation to achieve tension balance. It may be necessary to bypass tension disc altogether. Use in loopers only.
Monofilament Nylon	Very fine. Clear or smoke color. Variety of weights—#60 and #80 (finer) are common.	N, UL, LL (Use finer weights for needle.)	*	N		Strong, invisible thread, used with decorative thread, may melt with hot iron. The higher the number, the finer the thread.	Fashion accessories, home decorator items requiring strong seams, thread invisibility.	Some brands are too heavy and wiry to loop well. Look for lightweight, supple selection.
Elastic	Various sizes, including 1/4 – 3/8" widths.	A SO-1/4" & 3/8" widths	*	S		Adds stability. Used for shirring.		
Machine Embroidery, Lingerie	Variety of colors.	N, UL	**	N-S		Lightweight, smooth, delicate.	Lingerie, lightweight fabrics where stress is not a factor. Edging soft fabrics.	

Most often the decorative thread is threaded through the upper looper. This part of the stitch shows on the top side as you serge. On a rolled edge (page 51) or reversible-edge binding (page 61), the upper looper thread should be the only thread visible on either side.

If you want a balanced stitch (identical on both top and bottom), you will also need to thread the lower looper with decorative thread. In some cases, when the thread is not strong, the lower looper will not be able to handle a thread that works in the upper looper. This is because the upper looper thread has less movement in the thread guides and a shorter distance between the spool and the presser foot, so less stress is put on the thread.

The loopers don't pass through the fabric, so they both have larger eyes than a serger needle. This makes it possible to use thicker thread or yarn in your loopers. Consider these questions in determining whether a thread or yarn will work in the serger loopers:

1. When folded over double-layer, will the decorative thread easily pass through the looper eye? (Fig. 2-5)

Fig. 2-5: *Be sure your decorative thread or yarn will easily pass through the looper eye when it is doubled.*

2. Is the thread flexible enough to form a uniform stitch without catching in the loopers?

3. Is the thread smooth or tightly twisted enough to ensure trouble-free feeding and prevent fraying or snagging?

4. Is the thread yardage continuous and long enough to complete the project? (Always allow an extra 8 to 10 yards for testing.)

Some lightweight threads also fit through the needle eye. Woolly nylon, fine metallic thread, lightweight monofilament nylon, and top-stitching thread are examples. These threads therefore can be used for the ladder side of flatlocking (see page 43) or for other stitches that require loosened needle tension. In many cases, though, you will not need decorative thread in the needle, so use all-purpose or serger thread.

If a yarn, ribbon, or trim is too heavy or wide to fit through a looper or needle, you have the option of serging over it. To do this, make sure that the stitch you use is wide enough to cover the trim without stitching into it. You also have the option of using a 3-thread balanced, rolled-edge, or flatlock stitch, so test first for the best results.

When serging over trim, use an optional presser foot designed to guide it accurately (see page 11) or insert the trim under the back of the presser foot and over the front. Make sure the trim fits to the right of the needle and to the left of the knife. Turn the handwheel to form 1" to 2" of stitches over the trim before

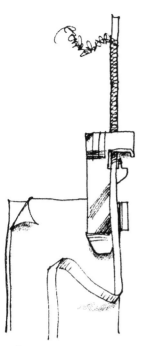

Fig. 2-6: Serge over trim for 1" to 2" before inserting the fabric.

inserting the fabric. (Fig. 2-6) Always serge slowly. To highlight the trim rather than the stitching, use monofilament nylon or matching lightweight serger thread in the upper looper.

If the trim is bulky, use a beading foot, or remove the presser foot and guide the trim manually between the needle and the knife. Hold both the trim and the fabric taut. As we discuss corded edgings and other techniques requiring serging over threads or strands, we'll give more specific instructions for successful results.

Special threading tips

To begin, clip the thread you are using above the spool and tie on the decorative thread. Bypass the tension control to prevent the knot from breaking or untying as it is pulled through. Pull the knot through the remaining thread guides. You may have to clip the knot at the eye of the looper or needle and thread it through manually.

Heavy or limp decorative threads are difficult to thread through the looper eyes. Serger pros use several tricks to do the job easily. Naomi makes a thread cradle by looping a strand of all-purpose thread around the specialty thread and then threads the ends of the all-purpose thread through the eye. (Fig. 2-7)

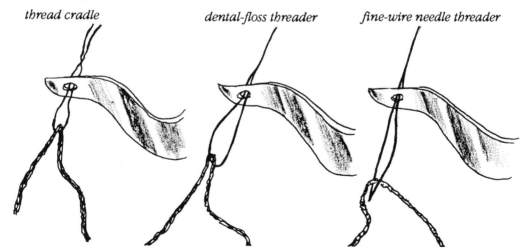

thread cradle *dental-floss threader* *fine-wire needle threader*

Fig. 2-7: Options for easily threading heavy or limp decorative threads through looper eyes.

Tammy uses a dental-floss threader (available at any drugstore) for the same purpose. Fine-wire needle threaders are also available from sewing retailers and mail-order sources to simplify the threading process.

Rethread the tension control and start serging with wide, long stitches. Gradually test and alter the stitch for the desired effect. For the most accurate results, always test on scraps of actual project fabric.

Turn the handwheel a few stitches to make sure the stitches are forming correctly. Then serge slowly for a few inches before stopping to adjust the tension. One general rule to keep in mind: the more resistance a thread has, the less tension it needs to have exerted on it. For example, a rough metallic thread needs less (looser) tension and a smooth, shiny rayon needs more tension.

If the tension is too tight after loosening it all the way, check to be sure the thread hasn't become hung up on a thread guide. If it is still too tight, remove the thread from the tension control or a pincher guide. For lay-in tension discs, place a strip of transparent tape over the tension slot to keep the thread out. (Fig. 2-8)

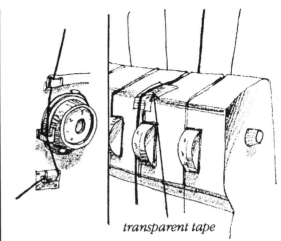

transparent tape

Fig. 2-8: *If the tension is too tight, remove the thread from the tension discs. For lay-in discs, place transparent tape over the slot to keep the thread out.*

S **Special Tip:** Tensions and stitch length can vary from machine to machine, even on the same model. Your dealer cannot expand the range but can adjust it slightly in one direction or the other.

Adjust to the desired stitch length. Most decorative seams and edges are serged with a very short "satin" stitch length. There should be enough thread coverage so little, if any, fabric shows through the serging. But, **if you adjust the serger for too short a stitch length, the fabric may jam under the presser foot** or the seam may pucker. To be safe, we usually begin with a medium (3mm) stitch length (especially for heavier decorative thread) and adjust toward a shorter length as far as necessary for the most attractive satin stitch. The thickness of the thread and the type of fabric you use will determine how short a stitch length you need. Finer thread requires a shorter stitch length for maximum coverage, while heavier thread

short stitch length—
finer thread

longer stitch length—
heavier thread

Fig. 2-9: *For maximum coverage, use a shorter stitch length when using finer thread. Lengthen the stitch slightly for heavier thread.*

looks better with a slightly longer stitch length. (Fig. 2-9)

When shortening the stitch length, you will also need to tighten both looper tensions or the stitching will hang off the edge of the fabric. (Fig. 2-10)

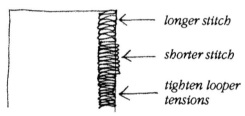

← longer stitch

← shorter stitch

← tighten looper tensions

Fig. 2-10: *Tighten both looper tensions when shortening the stitch so stitches won't hang off the edge.*

Because decorative stitching is an important part of the design of a garment or project, the stitches must be smooth and uniform. The slightest pulling of the decorative thread can narrow the stitch or even break the strand. (Fig. 2-11)

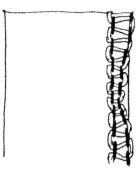

Fig. 2-11: *Stitches will narrow or break if the decorative thread does not feed evenly.*

If uneven stitches are a problem, check for anything that may be causing uneven feeding of your decorative thread. One common problem is that the thread catches on the spool itself (prevented by using a spool cap, usually in your accessory kit) or winds around the spool pin under the spool. Make sure the thread feeds evenly off the spool.

Use thread nets to control the feeding of slippery or wiry thread. For threads wound on balls or skeins, rewind the thread loosely by hand onto empty cones or spools. Rewind thread and yarn quickly with a cone-winder, sold in knitting shops.

Some serger pros prefer simply reeling off several yards of thread at a time from the ball or skein while serging. With this method, be sure that the feeding is not impeded by sewing tools cluttering your work area.

To illustrate how important even feeding can be, our serging friend Sue Green-Baker tells an amusing story. As she was working with decorative yarn in her upper looper, she kept getting uneven stitches (which she calls hiccups) in her serging. After checking all the usual trouble spots, she discovered that her kitten was playing with the ball of yarn on the floor. Even though she was reeling off extra yarn as she serged, the kitten's pulling occasionally caused just enough tension change to create major glitches in her otherwise perfect decorative stitching.

Combining thread types

You may need to make additional tension adjustments when you combine different thread types and use them in the same looper simultaneously. We do this for special decorative effects, such as adding a shiny fine metallic thread to woolly nylon or for toning down the color blocking of a variegated thread using one solid-color thread or another strand of the same thread with the colors aligned differently. Another thread commonly combined with a decorative one is fine elastic thread, because it adds stretch-prevention to serged edges and seams.

When combining thread types, make sure both are feeding evenly without restrictions. You may need to adjust the tension or remove one of the threads from the tension control. Always test first before serging your actual project.

Pressing over decorative thread

Some types of decorative thread (such as woolly nylon, monofilament nylon, and pearl cotton) are sensitive to a hot iron. For best results, use a press cloth to prevent melting or a permanent shine on

Troubleshooting with Decorative Thread

Problem	Cause
Uneven stitches or stitches narrow during serging	Thread feeding unevenly Thread catching on spool Thread winds around spool pin Incorrect spool holders used
Upper looper thread not pulling to edge of fabric	Looper tension too tight (see page 18) Lower looper tension too loose Stitch too wide Stitch too long Thread too heavy for stitch width
Stitches do not form	Threaded incorrectly Tension too tight Machine won't handle thread used Needle too small
Thread breaks	Thread inappropriate for serging Thread caught on thread stand, thread guide, or spool

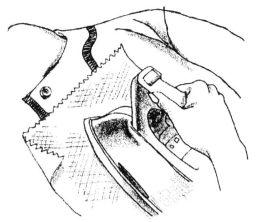

Fig. 2-12: *Use a press cloth to prevent melting or shine with sensitive decorative thread.*

your thread. (Fig. 2-12) Consider the fiber content of the thread and treat it similarly to a fabric of the same type. If in doubt, test first.

Threads Other Than Decorative

All-purpose or serger thread: All-purpose thread is most often cotton-covered polyester, wound parallel on conventional spools. Serger thread usually has the same fiber content but is lighter in weight than all-purpose thread. It is crosswound on cones or tubes so that it will feed more evenly, in an upward direction, during higher-speed serger sewing.

Monofilament nylon thread: Used for many serger techniques, this handy thread comes in either clear or smoke shades. We prefer the lighter-weight size 80 thread for use in either the needle or loopers. Monofilament nylon is practically invisible for covering serger-applied trims and for "floating" stitches on top of

the fabric. Because the nylon also is strong, you can use it in the lower looper for tightening down a rolled edge or for perfecting other techniques. Be careful to prevent melting this thread when pressing.

Fusible thread: A special thread combined with a heat-activated component, this exciting product bonds easily at the touch of a steam iron (much like fusible interfacing). Fusible thread helps stabilize and position edges and seam allowances in a wide variety of decorative techniques. We also use it to position serged braid or cord for couching and monogramming. Always test your application first on your project scraps.

Although top-stitching may be added for extra security, the pliable fusible thread bond withstands both washing and dry cleaning. For maximum fusing coverage, we usually use it in the lower looper of a 3- or 4-thread serged stitch. The more fusible thread exposed, the better the bond. When you use this thread in the lower looper, tighten the tension slightly so the thread does not extend past the edge of the fabric.

Always press from the top side of the stitching. Never allow the iron to touch the fusible thread directly. Because the fusible component has a low melting point, press-baste first with a warm iron. Then permanently bond using as much steam and heat as your fabric will tolerate. Allow the bond to cool before moving the fabric. Also, quickly secure seam ends with a shot of steam applied over (but not touching) the thread chain.

Shaping Materials

Clear elastic: About one-third the thickness of regular elastic, clear polyurethane elastic does not "grow" as it is stitched through. It is also impervious to nicks from serger knives. Handy for many sewing and serging projects, it comes in five widths—1/8", 1/4", 3/8", 1/2", and 3/4".

Elastic thread: Available in a range of colors and sizes (from lightweight to cording), elastic thread has several interesting serger applications. All but the heaviest weights can be threaded through the loopers. Elastic thread can also be used to create shirring or to stabilize an edge.

Fishline: If you don't already have some on hand, fishline is available at most sporting goods, discount, and drug stores. We use it for decoratively ruffling edges. Choose the clear line to avoid show-through in your project. Fishline weights vary from 12 lb. to 40 lb. Use the 12 lb. for lightweight fabrics and a heavier weight for heavier fabrics, when serging over two layers, or for extra body.

Fine wire: Wire, used to shape ornamental edges, is available in any craft store. Fine, lightweight floral wire is usually precut to 18" lengths. For projects that require longer lengths, try beading wire, which comes on spools and in a variety of colors and weights.

Batting: Various weights of batting are available in both cotton and polyester. We prefer either bonded batting, which holds together well, or fleece, which is thinner.

Fiberfill: This shredded batting is most often polyester and is used to stuff pillows and in craft projects.

Other Important Serging Supplies

- Your serger

- Your owner's manual and all machine attachments

- The serger's accessory kit—often including tweezers for easy threading, a screwdriver for adjustments, oil and a lint brush for regular maintenance, thread nets and spool caps for smooth feeding of special threads, and a spare knife and needles for convenience. A rolled-edge foot or plate and other machine-specific items may also be included. Refer to your manual for detailed information.

- Optional accessory feet

- A straight-stitch sewing machine, preferably with zigzag capability

- Needle-nosed pliers or needle inserter

- Extra needles

- Extra knives

- Fine-wire needle threader or dental-floss threader

- Extra thread nets

- Seam sealant like *Fray Check*

- Washable glue stick or fabric glue (such as Aileen's *OK to Wash-It* or Magic American's *Fabric Mender Magic*)

- Fusible transfer web (such as *Wonder-Under*)

Fig. 2-13: *Keep a sample book of notes, test results, and creative ideas.*

- Stabilizers—both water-soluble (such as *Solvy* or *Wash-Away*) and tear-away
- Dressmaker shears
- Rotary cutter and mat
- Seam ripper
- Yardstick
- Tape measure
- Water-soluble and air-erasable marking pens
- Machine lint brush or canned air
- Loop turner, darning needle, or crochet hook
- Any other favorite sewing supplies

Ornamental Serging Sample Book

We recommend that you keep a sample book of all your lesson results and other testing for later reference. One perfect way to do this is to use an owner's workbook (available for many models) and add extra pages for additional samples. (Fig. 2-13) Or use a standard 3-ring binder with heavy paper to mount your finished samples.

Be sure to note your tension, stitch width, and stitch-length settings for each type of stitch, thread, and fabric used. This information will be handy as a starting point for your future projects.

Put creative ideas in your sample book, too. Clip magazine photos, write notes about techniques to try, and add special instructions that come with new types of thread or other ornamental serging supplies. Refer to your sample book for inspiration and information while planning and completing each new serger project.

Exploring Your Machine's Creative Limits

As you work through this book, you will no doubt come up with bright ideas of your own. Because serger sewing is a relatively new art, there are many techniques and ideas yet to be discovered and developed.

Be open to experimentation. Test new serger techniques. Think about how you can adapt them for your own use. Then take time to answer the following questions in order to inspire your creative efforts:

1. *How can I adapt new sewing products and threads for serger use?* With so many recent technical advances, new serging possibilities abound. Fusible thread (page 27) opened up a wealth of new techniques for us. Clear elastic and elastic thread (page 28) add even more options. Interesting new decorative threads (pages 20-21) continue to be introduced.

2. *How can I combine craft products and ideas with my serging skills?* Many of our latest techniques and projects have come from using craft items such as fine wire (Lesson 7), water-soluble stabilizer (Lessons 24 and 32), and beads (Lesson 28).

3. *Can I convert sewing techniques for the serger in order to speed up a project or make it more durable?* Fishline ruffles (Lesson 6), lettuced edges (Lesson 5), and French seams (Lesson 1) are a breeze with the help of a serger.

4. *Are there unique stitch configurations on the serger that I can use for unusual ornamental effects?* Serged lace (Lesson 24), reversible-edge binding (Lesson 8), and serger chain art (Chapter 8) were all developed because of the machine's unique stitching capabilities.

5. *Is there another way to manipulate an edge or a fold to get a different result?* Double-bound seams (Lesson 2) and edges (Lesson 13) and double rolled edges (Lessons 5 and 17) are some recent options.

6. *Can I copy a trim or decorative effect from ready-to-wear?* Look in stores, magazines, and catalogs for inspiration. Check out crafts projects, too.

The more you use your serger and experiment with all its ornamental options, the easier you will find it is to be creative and to develop ideas of your own. So start now to explore all of the machine's possibilities and really use it to its creative limits.

3. Decorative Seams

- **Lesson 1. Basic Seams**
- **Lesson 2. Serge-bound Seams**
- **Lesson 3. Flatlocked Seams**

Serging seams is one of the most basic uses for your serger. The type of fabric, the amount of stress placed on the seam during wearing, and personal preference are the most important factors in selecting which seam to use.

Any seam may be hidden on the inside or used ornamentally, exposed on the right side of the fabric. Exposed seams are especially popular on many of today's sportier ready-to-wear garments.

When seams are exposed, they become a decorative design element. Therefore, the tension and stitches must be perfect, no matter what kind of thread you use. Always test first with two layers of the project fabric and the same thread you will be using. Compare your samples with the illustrations of perfect stitch formation in your manual or on pages 5 through 8, and adjust accordingly.

When serging decorative seams, the method you use to secure seam ends is important. If a seam will be crossed by another serged seam, we usually don't secure the ends by any other method. The thread chain holds the fabric together until it can be seamed across and secured. If additional reinforcement is needed, we straight-stitch along the needleline of the second seam for about 2" to 3" across the first seam. (Fig. 3-1)

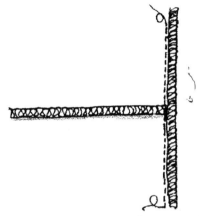

Fig. 3-1: *Serged seams are often secured by another seam. Straight-stitching can add reinforcement.*

When the seam ends will not be crossed and secured with a second serged seam, they must be secured by another method. The deciding factor is usually how much the method of securing will show. Because exposed seams are on the outside of the fabric and not worn next to the skin, our first choice is to use a drop of seam sealant on the ends. Be sure to let the sealant dry thoroughly before cutting the chain.

Special Tip: If the wet seam sealant accidentally touches another part of the project, leaving a stain, rub the spot with a cotton swab soaked in rubbing alcohol. The stain will disappear.

Lesson 1.
Basic Seams

When seaming, it is important to serge-trim some of the fabric, even if just enough to neaten the edges. This ensures even stitching, neater edges, and better control of the width trimmed. You'll find it easiest to trim between 1/8" and 3/8".

A basic serged seam can be sewn with either a 3-, 4-, or 5-thread stitch. If the seam will not be top- or edge-stitched but you want it to be as secure as possible, use a 4- or 5-thread stitch or straight-stitch along the needleline after serging a 3-thread seam.

Basic decorative seam

To serge a decorative, exposed seam, place the fabric wrong sides together and serge with the needle on the seamline. (When using two needles, the left needle will be on the seam line.) When both sides of the seam will show, use the same type of thread in both the upper and lower loopers. You may decide to use the same color for both loopers or to vary the colors to achieve a desired effect. Depending on the seam placement, you may not need to press (see our Nifty Knot Pillow project, page 36).

Exposed seams are often pressed to one side and top-stitched for neatness or to add strength. In this case, only the seam's upper looper thread will show. Apply top-stitching right next to the overlocked edge using a long stitch length. For better accuracy, use the blindhem foot on your sewing machine to guide your stitching evenly. Adjust the foot so that the overlocked edge is next to the guide. (Fig. 3-2)

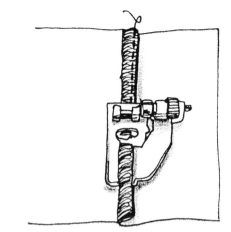

Fig. 3-2: *Use a sewing machine blindhem foot to top-stitch the decorative seam to one side.*

To secure an exposed seam quickly, put fusible thread (see page 27) in the lower looper when serging the seam. Before serging, determine to which side the seam will be pressed and serge with that side down. Tighten the lower looper tension slightly so the fusible thread does not show from the right side. Serge-seam. Carefully press-baste the seam to the side, then steam thoroughly to permanently fuse. For most seams, no other securing is needed.

Hidden lapped serging technique

We often need to lap decorative stitching—when completing a circle, joining the ends of an opening, or (occasionally) correcting irregular areas of serging. This technique eliminates the need to serge on and off the fabric and provides a neater (almost invisible) decorative finish.

1. Raise the needle(s) and presser foot and disengage the stitch from the stitch finger.

2. Insert your fabric, positioning the needle (left needle with a 4-thread stitch) on the seamline. If you are joining ends of an opening or correcting irregular serging, position the needle about 1/2" before the end of the left side of the opening. (Fig. 3-3)

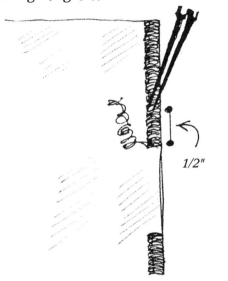

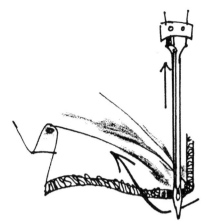

Fig. 3-4: Raise the needle(s) and presser foot and pull the fabric behind the needle(s).

Fig. 3-3: Position the needle(s) 1/2" before the end of the serging when closing an opening or correcting irregular stitching.

3. Serge until you reach the opposite end of the decorative stitching.

4. Overlap the stitches for 1/2", being careful not to cut the original stitching with your knives (disengage them if possible).

5. Raise the presser foot and needle(s), clear the stitch finger, and pull the fabric just behind the needle(s). (Fig. 3-4)

6. Serge off to form a thread chain.

7. If you're using a heavy decorative thread, dab on a drop of seam sealant and trim the chain when dry. If you're using a satin stitch and a lighter-weight decorative thread (such as woolly nylon), lapping the stitches should secure them adequately. Simply trim away the excess thread chain after lapping the stitches.

If you are lapping decorative serging and plan to trim the edge, trim away a 2" section of the seam allowance to the serger cutting line where you plan to begin your serging. (Fig. 3-5) Then position the cutting line against the blade before starting.

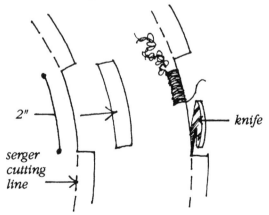

Fig. 3-5: When trimming the edge, cut away 2" to position the knife on the cutting line.

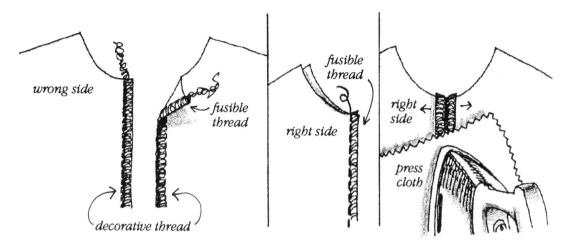

wrong side

fusible thread

decorative thread

fusible thread

right side

fusible thread

right side

press cloth

Fig. 3-6: *Serge-finish both edges from the wrong side. Straight-stitch, wrong sides together, along the needlelines. Fuse the allowances to each side.*

Reversed decorative seam

This attractive seam features decorative serge-finished allowances that are reversed to the right side of the garment and fused or top-stitched in place.

1. Adjust for the widest, satin-length, balanced, 3- or 3/4-thread stitch, using decorative thread in the upper looper, fusible thread in the lower looper, and all-purpose or serger thread in the needle. Tighten the lower looper tension slightly so no fusible thread shows on the top side of the stitching. Test first on project scraps.

2. Decoratively serge-finish both seam edges from the wrong side, positioning the needle (the left needle on a 3/4-thread stitch) on the seamline.

 Special Tip: If your fabric has a tendency to stretch, use a positive differential feed (above 1.0) or ease-plus manually.

3. Reverse the seam allowances to the right side of the garment by straight-stitching them wrong sides together along the needlelines, as shown. (Fig. 3-6) Use a zipper foot for accuracy.

4. Using a press cloth, fuse the allowances to the right side of the fabric on both sides of the seamline.

Optional: Use all-purpose or serger thread in the lower looper of the decorative stitching instead of fusible thread. After reversing the seam, press and top-stitch the allowances to both sides of the seamline instead of fusing.

Lapped seam

A lapped seam is formed by serge-finishing the edges of both layers of fabric separately, then top-stitching one to the other. Serge-finish both layers with the needle on the seamline. Overlap the edges, matching the seamlines. Top-stitch on the needleline, then top-

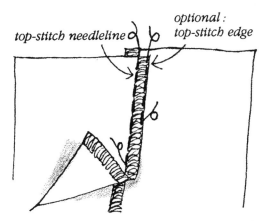

top-stitch needleline

optional: top-stitch edge

Fig. 3-7: *For a lapped seam, serge-finish both edges. Top-stitch them together along the needleline. Top-stitch again on the edge if desired.*

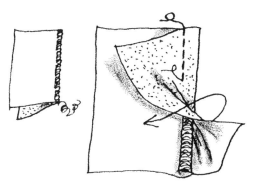

Fig. 3-8: *For an exposed French seam, serge a narrow seam with the right sides together. Wrap the fabric to enclose the serging and straight-stitch.*

stitch along the opposite side of the seam if desired. (Fig. 3-7)

Lapped seams are flat and very durable and are popular for reversibles. The upper looper thread on the top fabric layer is the only exposed part of the seam. For reversibles, both layers are serge-finished with one upper looper thread exposed on each side of the garment and top-stitched on the matched needlelines only.

Decorative French seam

Serged French seams on the outside of a garment or project form a decorative detail resembling a tuck. With the fabric right sides together, serge a narrow, medium-length, 3-thread seam. Fold the wrong sides of the fabric over the seam and press carefully. Straight-stitch next to the cut edges, enclosing the seam. Use your sewing machine's blindhem foot to sew a perfectly even width, placing the fold of the seam next to the guide on the foot. This ornamental

French seam works best on straight seams. (Fig. 3-8)

Mock flat-felled seam

The mock flat-felled seam, simple yet durable, is used on heavy fabrics. Top-stitching with decorative thread adds ornamental interest to your finished project. Use the widest 5-thread seam, or straight-stitch the seam (right sides together) with a 5/8" seam allowance and serge-finish the edges together using a 3- or 3/4-thread stitch. (Fig. 3-9)

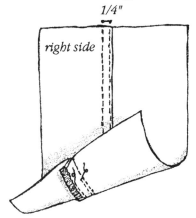

1/4"

right side

Fig. 3-9: *Create a mock flat-felled seam by serge-finishing wide allowances together, pressing them to one side, and top-stitching.*

Press the allowances to one side. For extra strength, use fusible thread in the lower looper when serge-finishing and fuse the allowances to one side. From the right side, top-stitch over the allowances right next to the seamline and again 1/4" away. Use a long stitch length and a decorative thread like buttonhole twist.

Project:
Nifty Knot Pillow

Exposed satin-stitched seams become a decorative detail on this attention-getting pillow. It's simple to serge and requires only 3/4 yard of fabric. (Fig. 3-10)

Fig. 3-10: *Feature decorative, seams-out detail on a novelty pillow.*

Foot: Standard
Stitch: 3- or 3/4-thread overlock
Stitch length: Satin
Stitch width: Widest
Thread: Contrasting color to fabric
   Needle(s): All-purpose or serger
   Upper looper: Decorative
   Lower looper: Decorative
Tension: Balanced
Needle(s): Size 11/75

Fabric: 3/4 yard 45"-wide solid, print, or crosswise-striped cotton or cotton blend
Notions: Polyester fiberfill

1. Cut two 13" by 45" rectangles.

2. Adjust your serger for a satin-length, 3- or 3/4-thread overlock stitch. (Fig. 3-11)

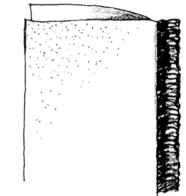

Fig. 3-11: *A satin-length, overlock stitch forms a pretty, textured seam.*

3. Raise the needle(s) and presser foot and clear the stitch finger. Place the two rectangles wrong sides together. Insert the fabric under the presser foot, positioning the needle(s) on the seamline 2" past the center of one long side (see the hidden lapped serging technique, page 32). Serge-seam all four sides, barely trimming the edges to neaten. Serge on and off at the corners and end the stitching about 5" from the beginning serging. Lightly stuff the pillow with fiberfill and serge-seam the opening closed using the hidden lapped serging technique.

4. Knot the pillow as shown.

Lesson 2.
Serge-bound Seams

One of the first things we learn about the serger is that it neatly finishes seams by overlocking the edges. Developing this feature further, we can vary the stitch length, width, and thread used to decoratively serge-finish seam allowances. We can also use the serger to speedily encase seam allowances in binding fabric.

Decorative serge-bound seams can be so attractive that we often choose to feature them on the outside of a project. This works especially well for jackets and coats because the seam allowance is featured ornamentally on the outside, while the inside shows only a neat seamline.

A professional-looking binding must be consistent in width. With the serger's exact cutting ability and the even width of its stitches, a consistent-width serged binding is almost foolproof.

Serged seam binding

This decorative seam finish is usually seen on the inside of unlined coats or jackets. It is easily achieved by finishing the seam-allowance edges with decorative, satin-length serging and then sewing the seam with a 5/8" seam allowance. (Fig. 3-12)

Adjust for a 3-thread stitch. Put a contrasting-color or tone-on-tone decorative thread in the upper looper. Adjust for a short stitch length and a medium to narrow stitch width. Serge-finish from the right side of the fabric, barely skimming the edge. We like to experiment with different stitch widths, depending upon the type of thread we use. Finer

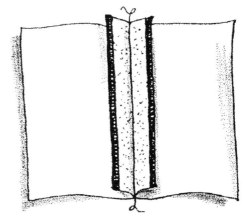

Fig. 3-12: *For serged seam binding, serge-finish the allowance edges with a satin-length stitch before seaming.*

thread needs more coverage and looks best with a narrow stitch width. Heavier thread is often more attractive in a wider stitch. Also try woolly nylon or glossy pearl rayon thread for attractive serged seam bindings.

Serged French binding

For a couture effect, add serged French binding to seams using a contrasting or matching strip of fabric. Try combining different types and colors of fabrics for stronger emphasis. Nylon/ *Lycra* works well as binding fabric because it folds tightly against the seam allowance. In addition, its bright colors can add a stunning contrast to dark or neutral fabrics. Try binding velvet with satin, wool with lightweight synthetic suede, or woven fabric with knits.

1. For a finished binding width of approximately 1/4", cut a binding strip 1" wide (four times the desired finished width). The width of the finished binding should be no wider than the width of your serger's widest stitch. If the seams to be bound are straight, the strip can be cut on the crosswise grain. However, if the bound seams are even slightly curved, cut woven strips on the bias or knit strips in the direction of greater stretch (usually crossgrain).

2. Adjust for your widest 3- or 3/4-thread stitch and a medium stitch length. From the wrong side, with fusible thread in the lower looper, serge-finish one long binding edge, trimming a scant 1/8".

3. Because the binding strip has a narrower seam allowance, it may be easier to pretrim the 5/8" fabric seam allowances to 1/4". Or serge the seam and trim it before applying the binding. As you become more comfortable with the application, you'll be able to serge-seam with a full seam allowance and apply the binding simultaneously. (Fig. 3-13) This one-step method is the easiest and fastest unless the fabric is difficult to manage. If the fabric is rigid, slippery, or must be held taut while serging, straight-stitch or baste the seam first and trim the seam allowances to 1/4" before applying the binding.

Place the right sides of the fabric together, aligning the binding strip on top over the seamline, fusible side down. (To position serged French binding on the outside of your garment, place the fabric wrong sides together.) Serge-seam the unfinished edges, leaving about a 1/4" seam allowance. The needleline of the serging should be on the seamline of the project. For accuracy, especially if your widest stitch is less than 1/4" wide, straight-stitch at 1/4" and serge-finish the edges together. (Serge-finishing the edges results in a smoother binding.)

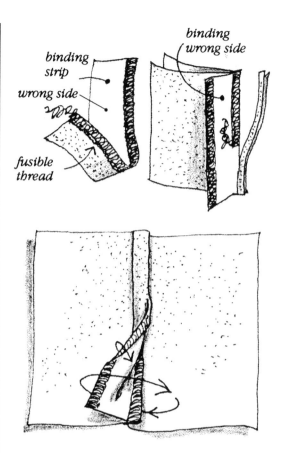

Fig. 3-13: *For serged French binding, finish the binding-strip edge with fusible thread in the lower looper. Serge-seam the binding and fabric together. Wrap the binding around the seam allowance and fuse it in place.*

If desired, you may change back to serger thread in the lower looper before serge-seaming. Do not stretch while seaming straight binding. For outer curves, ease the binding slightly, and for inner curves stretch it slightly. Wrap the binding smoothly around the seam allowance to encase it. Carefully press-baste to position the binding, then steam-press to fuse securely.

If you are applying a French binding without fusible thread, it is not necessary to serge-finish one long edge of the binding. Serge-seam the binding to the fabric, wrap the binding around the seam allowance, press, and stitch-in-the-ditch. Trim the unfinished long edge of the binding close to the stitching on the underside. Press the binding to one side and top-stitch next to the folded edge to secure. (Fig. 3-14)

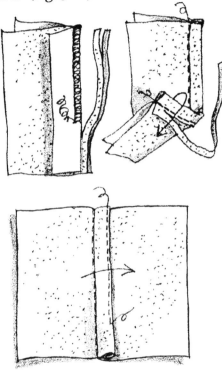

Fig. 3-14: *Make a French binding without fusible thread by serge-seaming the strip to the fabric. Wrap the strip around the seam allowance and stitch-in-the-ditch. Trim the unfinished edge, then top-stitch the binding to one side.*

Double-bound seam

This type of self-bound seam takes some extra time and skill to construct, but it is very durable and a real show-stopper. Both seam allowances are wrapped with self fabric, then decora-

tively serged from the right side. Using your widest 3- or 3/4-thread stitch width, the finished decorative seams will be about 1/2" wide. We will adapt this double-binding method for edges and decorative detail in later lessons.

1. To allow the extra fabric needed for wrapping a 1/4" seam allowance, before cutting out your garment or project, add an additional 1/2" to each edge that will be bound.

2. With right sides together, straight-stitch a seam using the seam allowance recommended on your pattern. (The seam allowance is usually 5/8" but may be 1/2" on home decorating projects.)

3. Press the seam allowances open and trim one allowance to a scant 1/4". From the right side, wrap the fabric securely around the trimmed allowance, forming a scant 1/4" fold. Press. (Fig. 3-15)

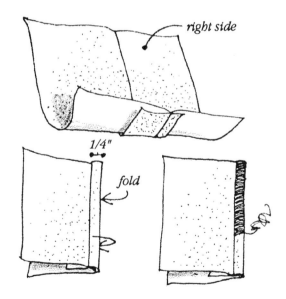

Fig. 3-15: *Make a double-bound seam by trimming the right seam allowance and wrapping the fabric around it. Serge-finish the fold.*

Special Tip: To minimize bulk on fabrics that do not ravel easily, try trimming the seam allowance to 1/8" before wrapping, then still press a scant 1/4" fold.

4. Use decorative thread in the upper and lower loopers and serger thread in the needle(s). Adjust for your machine's widest, satin-length, 3- or 3/4-thread stitch. If your widest stitch is narrower than 7.5mm, adjust the width folded so that the serged stitch will cover the entire fold. Test first.

5. Serge along the fold from the right side of the fabric, being careful not to cut it. The needle (the left needle on a 3/4-thread stitch) should be on the seamline. Adjust the tension so the overlocked stitches are tight against the fold.

6. Repeat steps 3 to 5 for the other seam allowance. When serging, make sure the needle stitches are right on or just inside the needleline of the first row of serging. (You will be serging in the direction opposite the first row of serging.) (Fig. 3-16)

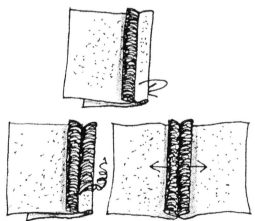

Fig. 3-16: Trim, wrap, and serge the other allowance, overlapping the needlelines. Press the allowances open.

7. Press the seam allowances open on the right side of the fabric. Use a press cloth, if necessary, to prevent melting the thread or leaving a shine.

 Optional: If you will be securing the finished double-bound seam to the fabric, use decorative thread in the upper looper only. Use serger thread in the needle(s) and lower looper. Top-stitch along each side of the binding. Or you may choose to use fusible thread in the lower looper when serge-finishing the folds, so you can fuse the binding to the fabric.

Double-piped seam

For this variation of the double-bound seam, follow the same procedure but use a narrow, balanced stitch on the 1/4" folds. The seam allowance will need to be trimmed to 1/4" (not narrower) so that it will catch in the narrower decorative serging and not pull out.

Note: With this technique, part of the fabric will show between the two sides of the binding. With a narrow, balanced stitch, the needlelines will not overlap. (Fig. 3-17)

Fig. 3-17: The double-piped seam is a double-bound seam that is serged with a narrow, balanced stitch.

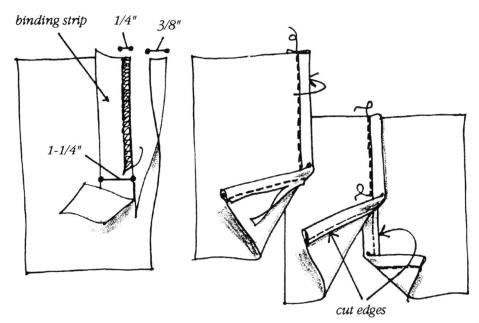

Fig. 3-18: *For a reversible lapped seam, serge-seam the binding to the allowances, wrap, and stitch-in-the-ditch. Trim the excess binding, then lap and top-stitch on the seamline.*

Bound and lapped seam

Construct a reversible lapped seam by serge-binding both edges and straight-stitching them together. Use reversible fabric or make the project of contrasting double layers with wrong sides together. The binding can either contrast with or match the fabric on each side. The bound edges are the width of the serged stitching, so use a narrower stitch width for a piped effect. (Fig. 3-18)

1. Cut two 1-1/4"-wide bias strips the length of the seam.

2. Trim the seam allowances to 1/4" or trim with the knives while serge-seaming the binding to each allowance. For contrasting binding, place opposite or contrasting sides together for serge-seaming. For a matching binding, place the same sides together.

3. After serge-seaming the binding, wrap the strip tightly around the serged allowances and stitch-in-the-ditch. Trim close to the stitching on the underside.

4. Lap the bound seams, matching the seamlines and sandwiching the trimmed binding edges between the two layers. Stitch-in-the-ditch over the previous stitching to complete the seam. Press flat.

Project: Reversible Hobo Bag

A bound and lapped seam is featured on this easy-to-make, reversible bag. Vary the pattern size for different uses or to suit your personal style. (Fig. 3-19)

Fig. 3-19: *This easy hobo bag features a bound and lapped seam and double straps.*

Foot: Standard
Stitch: 3- or 3/4-thread overlock
Stitch length: Short
Stitch width: Widest
Thread: Contrasting color
    Needles(s): All-purpose or serger
    Upper looper: Woolly nylon
    Lower looper: Woolly nylon, all-
        purpose, serger, or fusible
Tension: Balanced
Needle(s): Size 11/75
Fabric: 3/4 yard each of two contrast-
    ing 45"-wide water-repellent fabrics
    or soft upholstery fabrics
Notions: Four 1" D-rings; 20" of 3/4"-
    wide *Velcro;* 2 yards of 1"-wide
    cotton or nylon strapping

1. Cut two bag pieces from both fabrics using the pattern grid. (Fig. 3-20) Cut two 1-1/4"-wide bias strips the length of the lower edge of the bag. Piece if necessary.

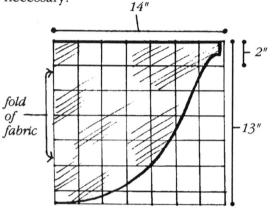

Fig. 3-20: *The hobo bag pattern grid—each square is 2".*

2. Place the wrong side of each bag piece to the wrong side of a contrasting piece. Bind the lower edges of both double-layer sides following the previous instructions. Lap and top-stitch the bound edges to 1-1/2" from each end, backstitching to secure.

3. Separate the *Velcro* and center it at the top of the bag with one side on the inside of the bag and the other on the outside of the opposite side (see Fig. 3-21). Adjust the stitch length and width to medium settings. From the right side, serge the top of both bag pieces, catching the *Velcro* in the stitching.

Special Tips: When serging with *Velcro,* do not use woolly nylon in the looper that carries stitches onto the *Velcro* piece. The woolly nylon's crimped fibers can catch on the *Velcro's* hooks and loops. Also test the stitch length first. You may need to lengthen the stitch when serging over *Velcro.*

4. Top-stitch the lower edge of the *Velcro* to each side of the bag.

5. Serge across the narrow ends with fusible thread in the lower looper. Wrap each end around a D-ring. Fuse and top-stitch to secure the D-ring. (Fig. 3-21)

Fig. 3-21: Secure the D-rings and straps by serge-finishing with fusible thread. Fuse them into position and top-stitch to reinforce.

6. Cut the strapping into two 36" lengths. Serge-finish each end with fusible thread in the lower looper. Insert each end of a strap through a D-ring. Fuse and top-stitch to secure.

Lesson 3. Flatlocked Seams

A flatlocked seam is always exposed on both sides of the fabric, so it can be used to add an interesting design detail. We most often see flatlocked seams on delicate lingerie and other garments on which sturdy seams are not essential. Although a flatlocked seam is relatively secure, it is not your best option for durability.

Perfecting flatlocking

The 2-thread overedge and 3-thread overlock stitches are most commonly used for flatlocking. A 2-thread flatlock uses less thread and therefore makes a finer, lighter-weight, and flatter seam. For both 2-thread and 3-thread flatlocking, loosen the needle thread tension so that the needle thread overlocks with the looper thread past the edge of the fabric. Because the needle thread is so loose, the seam can be pulled open until the stitches lie flat. (Fig. 3-22)

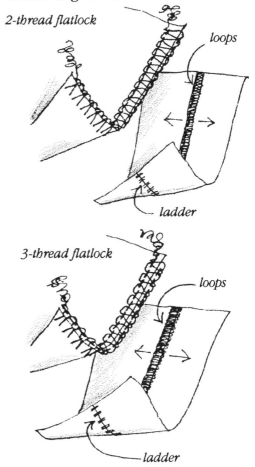

Fig. 3-22: To flatlock, loosen the needle thread. Allow the stitches to hang off the edge. Pull the stitches flat after serging.

The perfect flatlocked seam should be pulled completely flat. To do this, you must allow the stitches to hang off the edge as you serge. Feed the fabric under the presser foot slightly away from the knife. Your stitches will interlock beyond the edge, and you'll never have to worry about accidentally trimming your fabric. No amount of pressing will correct a flatlocked seam that cannot be pulled completely flat. Use the optional blindhem foot to guide the edge for an even flatlocked seam. Adjust the guide so the stitches will hang off the edge.

When flatlock-seaming, you must trim the edges before serging because your fabric is fed through slightly away from the knives so the stitches will hang off the edge. If you are flatlock-seaming a loosely woven fabric that will ravel and could pull out during use, serge-finish the cut edges first with a narrow, medium-length, balanced stitch using matching thread.

You may choose to have either the loops or the ladder side of a flatlock showing on the right side of your project (see Fig. 3-22). Both create a distinctive design detail. When flatlocking with decorative thread, keep in mind which part of your stitch will be exposed. Seaming with right sides together, the decorative thread must go through the eye of the *needle* if you want the ladder on the outside. But if the loops will be on the outside (seaming with wrong sides together), the decorative thread must be in the *lower looper* of a 2-thread flatlock and in the *upper looper* of a 3-thread flatlock. For additional details on decorative flatlocking, see Lesson 25 (page 118).

Reinforced flatlock seaming

We often use this durable flatlock seaming method. First straight-stitch the seam on your sewing machine. You may choose to serge-finish the edges before stitching. Fold on the seamline with the wrong sides together if you want the loops to show. Fold with right sides together if you want to feature the ladder stitches. Using your widest stitch width, flatlock over the folded seam. Pull the stitching flat. If you have not serge-finished the seam allowances, trim them close to the stitching. (Fig. 3-23)

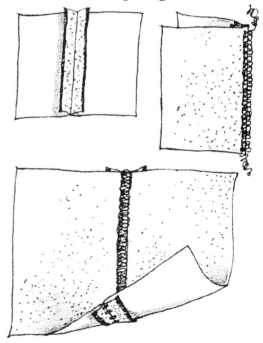

Fig. 3-23: *For reinforced flatlocking, straight-stitch the seam. Fold the fabric and flatlock over the seamline.*

Optional: Eliminate the straight-stitching step by pressing the seam allowances back and placing them together. Flatlock over the folds and pull flat. This also makes a durable flatlocked seam.

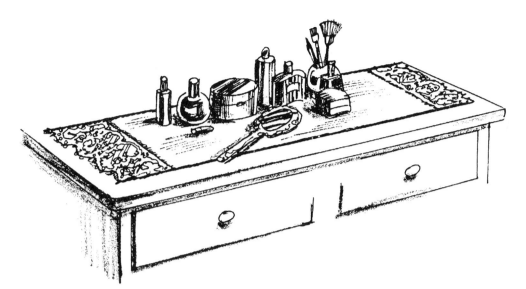

Fig. 3-24: *For an attractive dresser scarf, simply flatlock lace to the short edges of a fabric rectangle and serge-finish the long edges.*

Test each fabric or combination of fabrics before you flatlock. You may need to adjust tensions to accommodate the different thicknesses of your fabric. After flatlocking lace to tricot, for example, you may have to readjust your tensions before flatlock-seaming two layers of tricot.

Project: Lace-trimmed Dresser Scarf

Whip up a pretty dresser scarf with only a short length of fabric and a yard of lace. (Fig. 3-24)

Foot: Standard
Stitch: 3-thread flatlock for attaching lace; 3-thread overlock for serge-finishing
Stitch length: Medium to long for flatlocking; short to medium for serge-finishing
Stitch width: Medium to widest for flatlocking; narrow to medium for serge-finishing

Thread: Matching color
   Needle: All-purpose, serger, or machine embroidery
   Upper looper: Lightweight rayon or serger
   Lower looper: Serger or machine embroidery
Tension: Flatlock for attaching lace; balanced for serge-finishing
Needle: Sharp, size 11/75
Fabric: 3/8 yard of 45"-wide linen or cotton/polyester
Notions: 3/4 yard 3/4"-wide lace with one flat side

1. With wrong sides together, flatlock half of the lace to each short end of the scarf.

 Optional: For a narrower dresser or chest, shorten the scarf to 3" less than the dresser width before attaching the lace.

2. Serge-finish both long ends, including the ends of the lace. Dab the corners with seam sealant to secure.

4. Decorative Edges

Finishing edges is a basic serger function. In fact, it is the only way some home-sewers use the serger. But edge-finishing can go way beyond the basics. By making simple tension changes and using decorative thread, you can transform edges into an ornamental element. When decoratively serge-finishing, it is important to consider how you will use the finished garment or project. If an edge will receive stress during use or wear, it must be stabilized in some way during construction or finishing. The stabilizing technique may be inconspicuous or decorative. Always test first with the thread and actual fabric you will be using.

When testing, look for stretching of the edges after they have been serge-finished. To prevent this, you may need to serge over a stabilizer such as elastic, cording, water-soluble stabilizer, or decorative trim. Or you may choose to serge over the fold of the fabric (see pages 54 and 67). Decorative serged bindings (featured in Chapter 5) will also stabilize an edge.

Check to see if the decorative serged stitch will pull away from the edge easily. (This occurs most often on chiffon and loosely woven or bias fabric.) If it does, you may need to lengthen or widen the stitch, serge the edge over water-soluble stabilizer, try another kind of decorative edge, or save the fabric for another project.

Lesson 4. Balanced Decorative Edges

As soon as you've mastered tension adjustment, you're ready to embellish your garments and other projects with simple ornamental edges. If just the top edge will be exposed on a balanced stitch, use decorative thread in the upper looper only. If both sides of the serging will show, use decorative thread in both loopers. (Fig. 4-1)

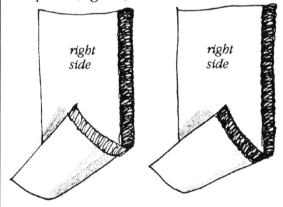

Fig. 4-1: *On a balanced edge, use decorative thread in the upper looper if only the right side will be exposed. When both sides will show, use it in both loopers.*

When decoratively serging curved edges, use a medium or narrow width for easier handling and a neater stitch. If you plan to trim the edge while serge-finishing, clip away 2" of the seam allowance (along the serger cutting line) where you will begin and end the serging. (See the instructions for the hidden lapped serging technique, page 32.)

When serging outside corners, we usually simply serge off the fabric at each corner and then serge back onto the adjoining side. Most often, we secure the thread chain at each corner with seam sealant and clip the tail when dry. This method eliminates any pretrimming if your project seam allowances are wider than the finished serged stitch.

Serge-scalloped edge

Your sewing machine and serger can team up to create some unusual ornamental effects. If your sewing machine has a variety of decorative stitches, try different ones in combination with a serged edge. Most sewing machines have a blindhem stitch that can be used to add a scalloped edge to your project. In testing, we have found that this technique works best on a folded edge or two layers of light- or medium-weight fabric.

1. Serge-finish the edge. Use the same thread in both the upper and lower looper for ease in scalloping. To begin testing, adjust for a satin stitch length. The width of the stitch and the appearance of the scallops will vary with the weight of the fabric. Use your widest 3-thread stitch for medium- to heavy-weight fabrics and a narrower width for lightweight fabrics. (Fig. 4-2)

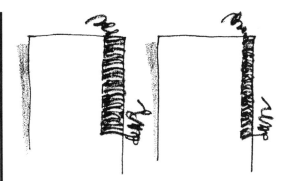

Fig. 4-2: Use a wide stitch for medium- to heavy-weight fabrics. Use a narrower stitch for lightweight fabrics.

2. Thread your sewing machine with thread matching the serged edge and adjust it for a blindhem stitch. Set the stitch width the same or slightly narrower than the serge-finished edge. With the serging to your left and the body of the fabric to your right, blindhem stitch the edge, allowing the zigzag of the stitch to go off the edge to form a scallop. You may have to tighten the needle tension slightly to make the edge more scalloped. Adjust the stitch length to test different sizes of scallops before finishing the garment edge. (Fig. 4-3)

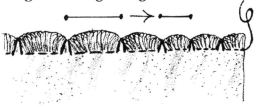

Fig. 4-3: Test the length of a sewing machine blindhem stitch to create the desired size of scallop.

Special Tip: When using the blindhem stitch to scallop the edge of a project, you must feed the bulk of the fabric through the machine to the right of the needle. To avoid having to do this, use your machine's shell stitch (reversible blindhem stitch) or a scalloping stitch if you have one. These stitches will create the same effect, but the bulk of the fabric remains to the left of the needle.

Serge-corded edge

Serging over filler cord (such as one or more strands of heavier thread, string, or cording) creates a corded overlock that can be used to stabilize a serged edge and add durability. The diameter of the filler cord or the number of strands used will change the thickness of the serged edge. When decorative thread and a satin stitch length are also used, the serge-corded edge becomes an attractive ornamental feature.

When serging over filler cord, it is important to guide the cord carefully between the needle and the knife without stitching or cutting it, making sure that the upper looper goes cleanly over the top of the filler. If your standard presser foot does not have a cording guide and you don't have an optional foot for that purpose, place the filler under the back and over the front of the foot, against the left side of the knife guard. (Fig. 4-4)

Begin serging over the filler cord by turning the hand wheel to make at least one stitch. Then begin serging at a slow speed to make sure that the cord is feeding correctly. Allow several inches of the filler to extend at the beginning and end of the serging.

To stabilize the edge, or when serge-cording around a curve, pull up on the filler to ease in the serged edge. Then knot securely. But remember, the rigid filler cord eliminates any stretch of the serged stitch.

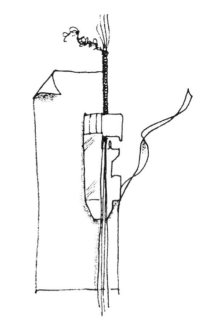

Fig. 4-4: *Serge over filler to create a corded edge.*

To simplify the application of filler cord, use either a beading/pearl/sequin foot or a ribbon/tape foot (see page 12). (Fig. 4-5)

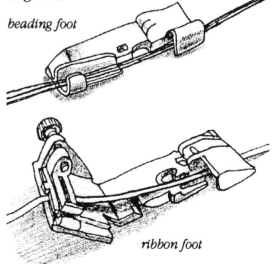

beading foot

ribbon foot

Fig. 4-5: *Use a beading foot or ribbon foot to simplify filler-cord application.*

Thread a **beading foot** according to the accompanying instructions. The filler feeds on top of a front guide and under a back guide. With a 3/4-thread model, either the right or left needle may be used, depending on the size of the filler. Use the left needle for larger, wider filler.

Thread a **ribbon foot** according to the instructions provided. The filler goes through a front guide and down under the back. You can also use either needle for the ribbon application, but we usually prefer the left needle because of its wider stitch capability.

After attaching either a beading or ribbon foot and selecting the appropriate needle, place the filler through the guides and serge onto it for several inches before inserting the fabric. Hold the cord taut (and toward the right side of the needle, if necessary) as you serge over it.

After completing the application, lift the presser foot and draw the unattached filler tail under the foot to the left before chaining off. (Fig. 4-6)

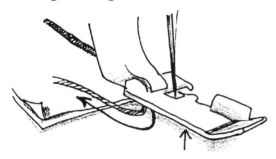

Fig. 4-6: *To chain off separately from the filler, lift the foot and draw the filler tail behind the needle.*

Serge-corded variations:

■ For an interesting ornamental effect, use monofilament nylon thread in the upper looper and a decorative filler.

■ For a thick, beefy, serge-corded edge, use several strands of matching-color filler cord. Adjust for a narrow, balanced stitch and a short stitch length to replicate manufactured cording.

■ For a cording that gives with the fabric as well as stabilizes, use elastic cording or 1/8" transparent elastic for filler. The elastics are especially good for serged filler cording on sweatering, interlocks, and other knits.

Picot-braid edge

Serging along a finished edge with a picot-braid stitch creates a distinctive looped edging for a cuff or collar. When serged from the wrong side of the fabric, only a dainty row of picot stitches shows from the right side. When serged from the right side, the entire width of the stitch is visible. (Fig. 4-7)

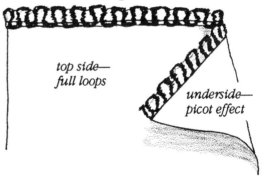

top side— full loops

underside— picot effect

Fig. 4-7: *Serge a picot-braid edge from either the right or wrong side with the needle just catching the fabric.*

1. Put a heavier decorative thread in the upper looper, monofilament nylon in the lower looper, and matching all-purpose or serger thread in the needle. Adjust for the widest, longest, 3-thread stitch with a balanced tension. For maximum width, try removing the decorative thread from the tension discs (see page 24).

2. Serge a few inches of braid before inserting the fabric. Stitch along the finished edge with the needle just catching the fabric.

3. Chain off a few inches of braid after completing the edge. Fold 1/2" of the chain ends to the underside and hand-tack to secure.

Project:
Simple Smock Apron

Create a fast and easy apron featuring decorative serged edges. It has good spill coverage and shows off your serging skills at the same time. (Fig. 4-8)

Fig. 4-8: *Use balanced decorative serging on a quick smock apron.*

Foot: Standard
Stitch: 3-thread
Stitch length: Short
Stitch width: Medium

Thread: Matching or contrasting color
Needle: All-purpose or serger
Upper looper: Woolly nylon
Lower looper: Woolly nylon
Tension: Balanced
Needle: Size 11/75
Fabric: 1-1/8 yard of 45"-wide cotton or cotton/polyester
Notions: 1-1/2 yard of 1/2"-wide matching grosgrain ribbon

1. Cut two smock pieces using the pattern grid (Fig. 4-9). Also cut one 20" by 8" rectangle.

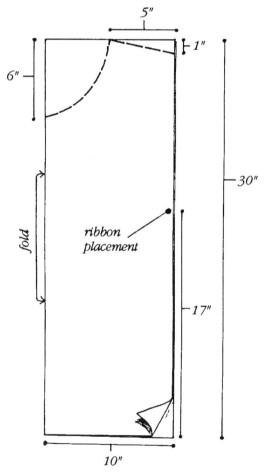

Fig. 4-9: *Smock-apron pattern grid.*

2. Serge-seam one shoulder with wrong sides together. Serge-finish the neckline edge, then serge-seam the other shoulder.

3. Serge-finish one long edge of the rectangle. Place the rectangle (with the finished edge up) on the right-side lower edge of one smock piece, matching the cut edges. Top-stitch down the center of the rectangle to form two pockets.

4. Curve the lower corners of both smock pieces, using a plate as a guide.

5. Cut the ribbon into four 13" pieces. Pin each ribbon to the wrong side of each smock piece at the placement marks.

6. Beginning at one ribbon placement, decoratively serge-finish the entire outer edge, being careful not to serge over the pins. To begin and end the decorative edge neatly, use the hidden lapped serging technique on page 32.

Lesson 5.
Rolled Edges

The narrow rolled edge (or hem) makes a wonderful finish for most light- and medium-weight fabrics on projects as varied as napkins and expensive dresses. With some adjustments, you also may be able to use a rolled edge on heavier fabrics. A rolled-edge finish may be either decorative or inconspicuous, depending upon the thread used. One

of the original selling points of the home serger was its ability to do a rolled edge more neatly, quickly, and easily than on a sewing machine.

Consult your owner's manual for instructions on converting to a rolled edge, because the process varies from model to model. On some, you will need to change a presser foot, needle plate, or both. On others, you will simply move or remove the stitch finger.

The only visible thread in a correctly adjusted 3-thread rolled edge is the upper looper thread. (Fig. 4-10) When

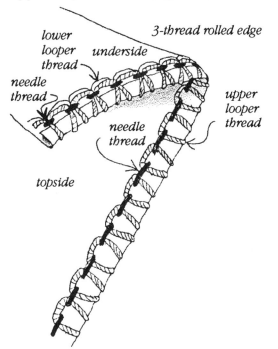

Fig. 4-10: *The upper looper thread wraps the edge. The lower looper and needle threads are barely visible.*

the tension is adjusted properly, the upper looper thread is pulled entirely around the edge of the fabric from needleline to needleline. The lower looper thread is tightened and forms a line that is almost straight. Both the lower looper and needle threads can barely be seen.

In a 2-thread rolled edge, the visible thread is the lower looper thread. (Fig. 4-11) It wraps the edge of the fabric

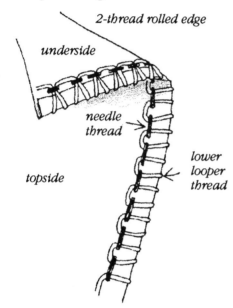

2-thread rolled edge

underside

needle thread

topside

lower looper thread

Fig. 4-11: *The lower looper thread wraps the edge. The needle thread is barely visible.*

from needleline to needleline much like the 3-thread version.

For both types of rolled edge, you will need only one spool or cone of decorative thread. With some decorative threads (and on certain fabrics), you may find it impossible to wrap the looper thread entirely around the edge using tension adjustment alone. A classic example is with slick rayon thread. Use woolly nylon or monofilament nylon thread in the lower looper on a 3-thread rolled edge or the needle of a 2-thread rolled edge. The added strength of the nylon will help roll the edge completely.

Loosen the tension on the monofilament nylon before starting to serge. If the tension is too tight, the monofilament thread may snap. Because it is practically invisible, monofilament is more difficult to rethread.

To form a rolled-edge stitch, the fabric must roll completely around the needle-like stitch finger. If your serger doesn't cut the seam allowance portion wide enough to wrap around the stitch finger, short threads may poke out through the stitching. (Fig. 4-12) Try these solutions to eliminate the problem:

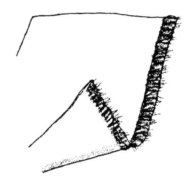

Fig. 4-12: *Threads may poke through the stitching on a rolled edge if the seam allowance is not wide enough to wrap to the underside or if the stitch is too long.*

1. Adjust your machine for a wider stitch, if possible. We find it easiest to start serging a medium stitch width, then gradually increase or narrow it as we test.

2. Shorten the stitch length to completely cover the edge with serged stitches.

3. Use monofilament or woolly nylon thread in the lower looper.

4. Place a strip of water-soluble stabilizer over the fabric edge before rolling it. Tear away the excess stabilizer after serging.

5. Press 1/4" to the wrong side and serge the rolled edge over the fold (see Serge-a-fold, page 54).

 Note: If threads extend beyond the stitching on the underside (rather than poking out to the side), adjust the knife, if possible, to narrow the bite. (Fig. 4-13)

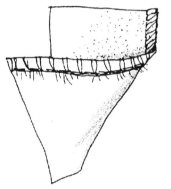

Fig. 4-13: Adjust the knife for a narrower bite if threads extend beyond the stitching on the underside.

Wiry fibers in your fabric or serging on the crosswise grain may also cause threads to poke through, but making the adjustments listed previously will usually correct the problem.

When serging loosely woven or light-weight fabrics, the rolled edge may pull away from the fabric. This occurs most often when serging with a short stitch length. If this happens, lengthen the stitch slightly. You may have to widen the bite, too. The grainline of the fabric may also be a factor when the edge separates from the fabric. Test-serge on both the lengthwise and crosswise grains, as well as on the bias.

Lettucing

Lettucing the edge is a finish used only on fabric that will stretch, such as knits and bias wovens. To make a ruffled lettuce edge, you must stretch while serging, using a very short (satin) stitch length. (Fig. 4-14) Be careful not to

Fig. 4-14: Lettuce the edge of a stretch or bias fabric by stretching while serging.

bend the needle while stretching the fabric. If you have differential feed, adjust it to its lowest setting to help with the stretching.

Because the fabric is stretched while serging, you may need to widen the bite, if possible, to allow enough fabric to roll over the stitch finger.

Double rolled edge

Two rows of rolled edge serged directly next to each other make an unusual ornamental detail that is also very durable. Use two contrasting thread colors, or try two different thread types for a heightened effect.

1. Serge the wrong side of one edge of the fabric with a satin rolled edge, leaving several inches of thread chain. (Fig. 4-15) Woolly nylon or a heavier rayon will provide the maximum thread coverage.

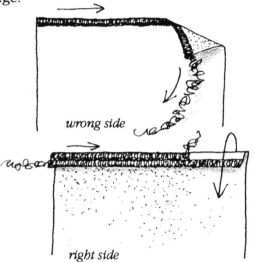

wrong side

right side

Fig. 4-15: *Create a double rolled edge by serging one row from the wrong side. Then fold the stitching to the right side and serge the second row on the fold.*

2. Rethread the upper looper with a contrasting thread.

3. With right sides together, refold the fabric next to the first rolled edge, leaving just enough width for another rolled-edge seam allowance.

4. Holding the thread chain to prevent jamming, serge a second rolled edge over the fold with the needle right next to the needleline of the original stitching. (Fig. 4-15) You will be serging in the opposite direction from the first serging.

5. Carefully press the double rolled edge flat.

Scalloped rolled edge

The scalloped rolled edge is similar to the scalloped edge made using balanced stitching (page 47). This edge-finish is seen on the finest ready-to-wear lingerie. If you are using a scalloped rolled edge on nylon tricot, remember that tricot rolls to the right side. For the nicest rolled edge and the least frustration, serge the rolled edge from the wrong side.

Serge-a-fold

The rolled edge is a durable edge in itself. But if you prefer more body on the edge, are having trouble with threads poking through the stitching, or feel the serged edge may pull off a loosely woven fabric, press the edge 1/4" to the wrong side and serge the rolled edge over the fold. (Fig. 4-16) On the wrong side, trim the raw edge right next to the serging.

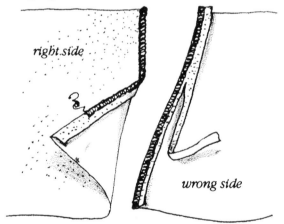

right side

wrong side

Fig. 4-16: *For durability and to eliminate threads poking through the stitching, serge over a folded edge. Trim the excess seam allowance on the wrong side.*

FISHLINE RUFFLES

CIRCULAR NECKLACES & BRACELETS

WOVEN SERGED STRIPS

Ornamental serging techniques add sophisticated interest to a classic ensemble. Fishline ruffles (Chapter 4), circular necklaces and bracelets (Chapter 8), and woven serged strips (Chapter 7) are subtly teamed to show off your serging skills.

TWISTED & HOOKED NECKLACES

SERGE- & -SEW STITCHING

SERGE- COVERED CORDING

Highlight a dress or top with serge-and-sew stitching (Chapter 7). Use serge-covered cording (Chapter 6) for the button loops, and accent the outfit with twisted and hooked necklaces (Chapter 8).

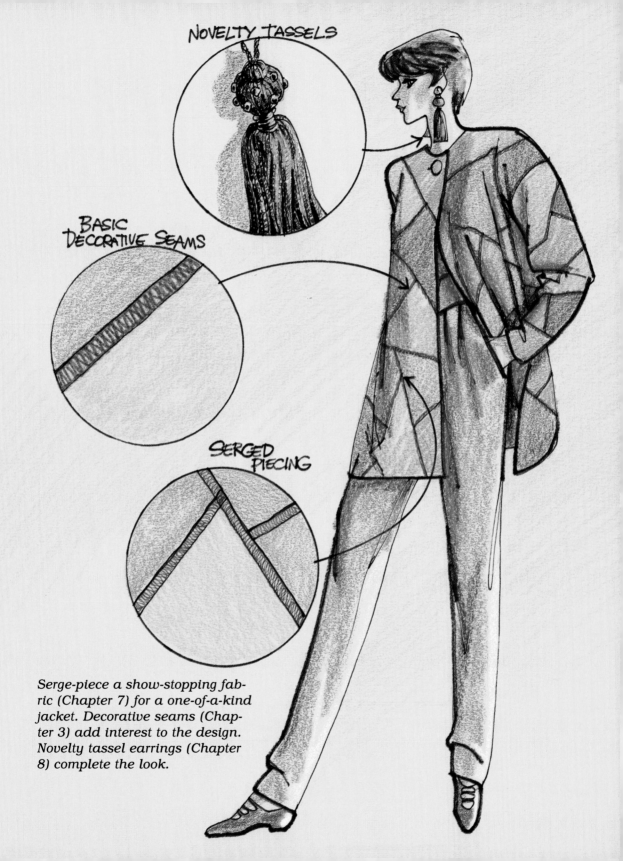

NOVELTY TASSELS

BASIC DECORATIVE SEAMS

SERGED PIECING

Serge-piece a show-stopping fabric (Chapter 7) for a one-of-a-kind jacket. Decorative seams (Chapter 3) add interest to the design. Novelty tassel earrings (Chapter 8) complete the look.

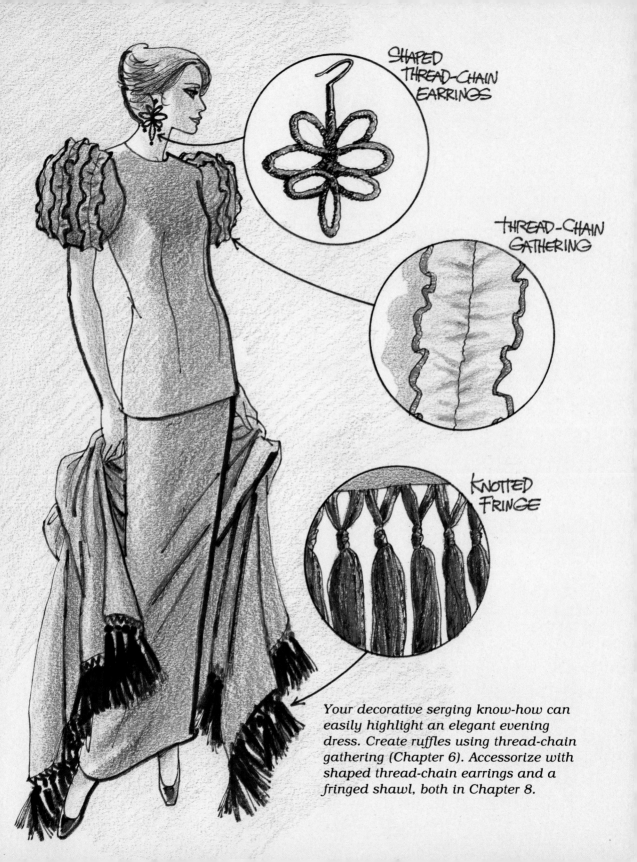

SHAPED THREAD-CHAIN EARRINGS

THREAD-CHAIN GATHERING

KNOTTED FRINGE

Your decorative serging know-how can easily highlight an elegant evening dress. Create ruffles using thread-chain gathering (Chapter 6). Accessorize with shaped thread-chain earrings and a fringed shawl, both in Chapter 8.

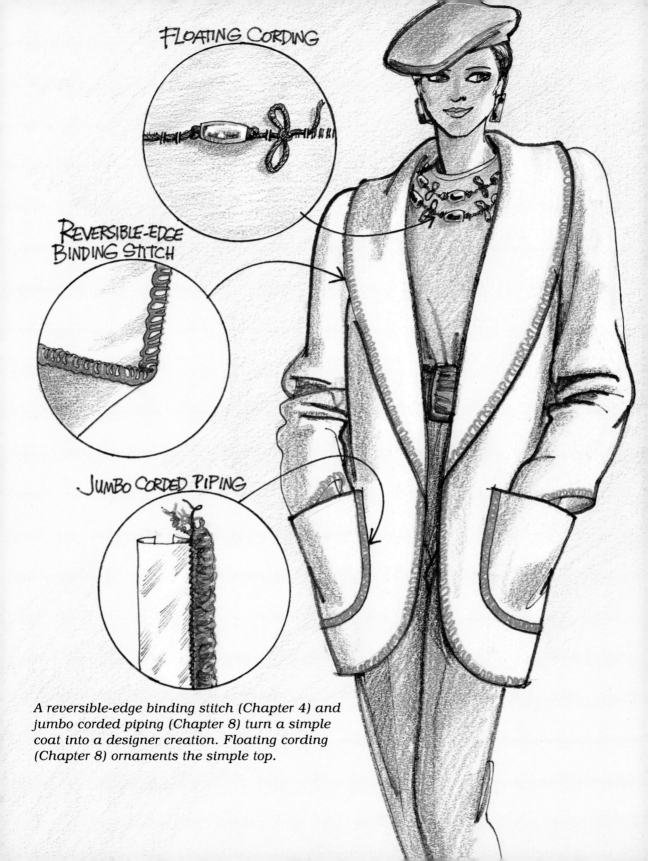

FLOATING CORDING

REVERSIBLE-EDGE
BINDING STITCH

JUMBO CORDED PIPING

A reversible-edge binding stitch (Chapter 4) and jumbo corded piping (Chapter 8) turn a simple coat into a designer creation. Floating cording (Chapter 8) ornaments the simple top.

FRIENDLY PLASTIC PENDANTS

BOUND & LAPPED SEAMS

PICOT ROLLED EDGE

Bound and lapped seams (Chapter 3) are featured on a lightweight reversible summer outfit. A picot rolled edge (Chapter 4) finishes the chiffon scarf, and Friendly Plastic pendants (Chapter 8) are used for the color-coordinated earrings and bracelet.

CORDED
FLATLOCK

FLOATING
FLATLOCK

DOUBLE
FRINGE

Turn any top into a fashion statement using both corded and floating flatlocking, as described in Chapter 6. Decorate a casual bag with double fringe (Chapter 8).

HEIRLOOM SERGING

FLATLOCKED LACE

SERGED ELASTIC BUTTON LOOPS

Underneath it all, your serger handles lingerie beautifully. Try heirloom serging (Chapter 7), flatlocked seaming (Chapter 3), and serged elastic button loops (Chapter 6) to accent a feminine teddy.

If the edge will be visible from both the top and underside, straight-stitch right next to the fold and trim the raw edge close to the stitching before applying the rolled edge.

For even more durability, combine serging on the fold with scalloped edging. If you are using a scalloped rolled edge on a single knit, the decorative stitch has a tendency to roll to the right side. To prevent this and add more body to the edge, serge-finish the edge with a narrow, balanced stitch, press 1/4" to the wrong side, and serge over the fold. Finish with the blindhem stitch to create scallops.

Picot rolled edge

This variation of the rolled edge is most often used on soft fabric such as tricot. It finishes the edges of lingerie garments and silky scarves beautifully. To make an attractive picot edge, simply alter a rolled-edge stitch (see page 51) for a long stitch length and tighten the upper looper tension slightly. (Fig. 4-17)

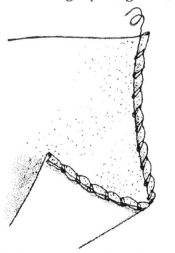

Fig. 4-17: *Serge a picot rolled edge by lengthening and slightly tightening the upper looper of a rolled-edge stitch.*

Project: Lettuced-edge Shawl

Wrap yourself in feminine chiffon on a special summer evening. (Fig. 4-18)

Fig. 4-18: *A large, lettuced-edge chiffon square makes an attention-getting summer wrap.*

Foot: Rolled edge or standard (depending on model)
Stitch: 3-thread
Stitch length: Satin
Stitch width: Medium
Thread: Matching or contrasting color
    Needle: All-purpose or serger
    Upper looper: Matching machine embroidery
    Lower looper: Monofilament nylon
Tension: Rolled edge
Needle: Size 11/75
Fabric: 1-2/3 yard of 60"-wide chiffon

1. Cut a bias square using the entire width and length of the fabric. (Fig. 4-19)

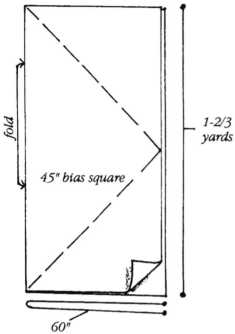

Fig. 4-19: Cut a bias square as large as possible.

Optional: Use 1-1/4 yard of 45" chiffon for a 30"-square ruffled scarf.

2. Serge-finish all four edges with a rolled edge, stretching as you serge. If available, adjust the differential feed to the lowest setting to help with the stretching. Apply seam sealant to the corners and clip the thread chains when dry.

Lesson 6.
Fishline Ruffles

The beautiful fishline ruffle, like its ready-to-wear forerunner, is most often seen on special-occasion garments and floral-like embellishments. Fishline is applied to the edge of the fabric similarly to filler cord, using a short- to medium-length, rolled-edge stitch. (Fig. 4-20)

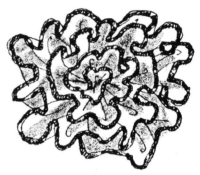

Fig. 4-20: Fishline ruffles add an unusual ornamental effect.

Fishline is available at most sporting goods, discount, and drug stores in weights varying from 12 lb. to 40 lb. The lighter weight is better for lightweight fabrics like tulle and netting. Use a medium weight (25 lb.) for fabrics such as satin and taffeta. Also use a heavier fishline if you are serging over two layers of fabric or if you want extra body. If you are edge-finishing a lightweight or sheer fabric such as tulle, be sure to use clear fishline.

Serging on bias fabric creates the prettiest ruffles, but on a loosely woven fabric the stitching may pull off. As an alternative, cut the fabric on the lengthwise grain.

While serging, it is important to guide accurately and **serge slowly.** If you accidentally cut the fishline while serging over it, you will need to rework part of your project. Use the techniques for serging over filler cord (page 48), guiding the fishline between the needle and the knives.

When serging over fishline, leave a long tail at the beginning and end of the serging (about half the ruffle length). First serge over the fishline for several inches, then place the fabric underneath. (Fig. 4-21) Do not stretch while serging. After serging, stretch for the amount of ruffling or flouncing desired.

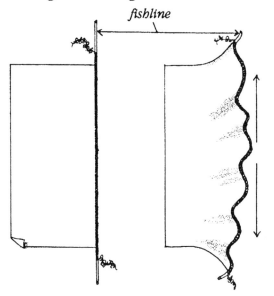

fishline

Fig. 4-21: *For fishline ruffles, serge over fishline, then stretch after serging.*

Project: Romantic Hair Ruffle

A fishline ruffle adorns the edge of this feminine hair ornament. (Fig. 4-22)

Fig. 4-22: *Use fishline ruffles on a fashionable hair accessory.*

Foot: Standard, rolled edge, or beading
Stitch: Rolled edge
Stitch length: Short
Stitch width: Narrow
Thread: Matching color
    Needle: All-purpose or serger
    Upper looper: All-purpose or serger
    Lower looper: Monofilament nylon
Tension: Rolled edge
Needle: Size 11/75
Fabric: 1/3 yard 45"-wide lace or 3/4 yard 45"-wide lightweight woven silky or chiffon
Notions: 3 yards clear 25-lb. fishline; 1/4 yard 1/2"-wide clear elastic

1. Cut a 12" by 24" rectangle from the fabric. Cut on the crosswise grain for lace or on the bias grain for wovens.

2. Finish both long edges by serging over the fishline, following the previous instructions. Stretch to ruffle.

3. Seam the short ends into a circle by straight-stitching with a short stitch length, back-stitching several times over the fishline to secure it. Serge-finish the seam allowances together close to the seamline.

4. Fold the fabric circle in half, with the top layer right side up and 1" shorter than the bottom layer, as shown. (Fig. 4-23)

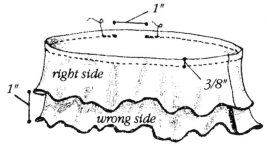

Fig. 4-23: *Fold the circle into a double ruffle and straight-stitch a casing in the center.*

5. Top-stitch 3/8" from the fold, leaving a 1" opening for threading the elastic.

6. Draw marks near the center of the clear elastic, 2-1/2" apart. Using a safety pin or bodkin, thread the elastic through the casing so that the marks are just outside the opening on either side. Knot the elastic securely together at the marks and trim the ends to about 1/2". Straight-stitch the opening closed.

Lesson 7.
Wire-shaped Edges

Much like fishline, fine wire can be used to shape serged edges. Unlike fishline, however, it is rigid and can be formed into almost any shape. (Fig. 4-24)

Fig. 4-24: *Fine wire shapes a delicate rolled edge.*

Fine wire is available in any craft store. We first used lightweight floral wire to shape edges of serged flowers and for serged-wire ornaments. Because most floral wire is precut to 18" lengths, we also now use fine beading wire, which comes on spools and in a variety of weights and colors.

When you serge a wire-shaped edge, it is essential that you guide the wire carefully and serge slowly. If you serge too fast, you may hit the wire with a needle, which could throw your serger out of alignment. Wire-shaped projects are for more experienced serger users, and even they need to be very careful.

Place the wire under the back and over the front of a rolled-edge foot or standard presser foot. If available, a beading foot (see page 11) can be helpful in guiding wire accurately. Carefully serge over the wire, keeping it between the needle and the knives.

When serging over wire, leave at least a 1" tail at both ends for securing. Begin by serging over the wire for at least one additional inch. Pull gently on the thread chain and the wire tail to guide the serging smoothly. Then raise the presser foot and position the fabric under the foot and wire. Serge slowly. After some fabric clears the back of the presser foot, bend the wire back over the fabric to anchor it during the remainder of the serging. (Fig. 4-25)

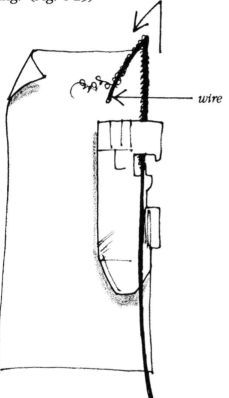

Fig. 4-25: Start serging over the wire, then insert the fabric. Bend the wire back over the fabric to anchor.

Project: Fancy Flower Pin

Use wire-shaped edges to make a pretty flower pin to brighten a lapel, hat, or handbag. (Fig. 4-26)

Fig. 4-26: A rolled-edge stitch over wire shapes an ornamental flower pin.

Foot: Standard, rolled edge, or beading
Stitch: 3-thread
Stitch length: Short
Stitch width: Narrow
Thread: Matching
  Needle: All-purpose or serger
  Upper looper: All-purpose, serger, or machine embroidery
  Lower looper: Monofilament nylon
Tension: Rolled edge
Needle: Size 11/75
Fabric: 1/8 yard of lightweight lace or chiffon
Notions: 20-gauge beading wire (found in craft stores); one small decorative button; one pin back (found in sewing and craft stores); glue gun

1. Cut seven 3" by 6" rectangles of the fabric with the 6" sides on the lengthwise grain.

2. Adjust for a rolled edge. Serge over wire on one long edge of each rectangle, following the previous instructions. Be sure to position the wire between the needle and the knives, serge over it for an inch or two, then feed the fabric under the presser foot. **Serge slowly.** At the end of each side, stitch over the wire for about an inch past the fabric, then lift the presser foot, pull the wire to the left behind the needle, and chain off. Leave at least 3" of wire on each end.

3. Serge-gather the other long edge of each rectangle, rounding the unfinished corners, as shown. (Fig. 4-27) Be sure to fold the wire out of the way of the knives when serging each end.

4. Shape the wire to form petals, and pull the needle thread (the shortest thread) of the serge-basting to gather the lower edge. Knot the basting threads, twist the wires together, and clip the thread tails.

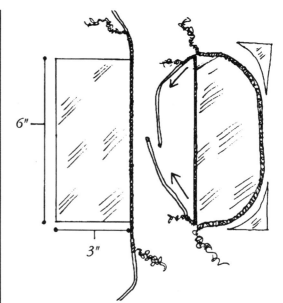

Fig. 4-27: Serge-finish one long petal edge over wire. Serge-gather the other long edge, rounding the corners.

5. To form a flower, place the seven petals right sides together and twist all the wires for about 1". Clip off the excess wire using wire cutters and bend the twisted section to one side. (Fig. 4-28)

Fig. 4-28: Shape the petals, pull up the basting thread, and twist the wires to secure. Twist together all seven petals to form a flower.

6. Using a glue gun, secure the raw edges of the petals on the underside of the flower and attach the pin back. On the top side, arrange the petals and sew the button in the center.

Lesson 8. Reversible-edge Binding Stitch

The upper looper thread wraps the fabric edge to form the reversible-edge binding stitch. Similar to the rolled-edge stitch, reversible-edge binding is used for heavier fabrics on which the edges do not roll under. Single-layer coats and blanket edges are common applications. Use heavier thread in the upper looper for a more durable edge.

For reversible-edge binding, use the standard presser foot and a medium-width, 3-thread stitch. On a 2-needle machine, use the right needle only.

Loosen the upper looper tension and tighten the lower looper tension. The thread should completely wrap the edge and look the same on both the upper and under side. (Fig. 4-29) If the thread does not wrap completely after loosening the tension, take the thread entirely out of the tension disc (see page 24) or the first thread guide. Narrowing the stitch width will also help wrap the edge.

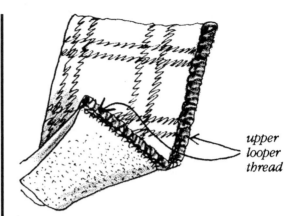

upper looper thread

Fig. 4-29: *For reversible-edge binding, loosen the upper looper and tighten the lower looper. The upper looper thread should completely wrap the edge.*

S **Special Tip:** If tension adjustments give a less-than-perfect stitch, switch to monofilament or woolly nylon in the lower looper. This strong thread often helps to wrap the stitch completely.

The reversible-edge binding stitch is a simple but decorative edge-finish, ideal for placemats, potholders, or cozies made from quilted fabrics. Before serging the edge of quilted fabric, compress the thickness by zigzagging over the area to be serged, using a long, wide stitch. Then serge directly over the zigzagging.

Fig. 4-30: *Decoratively bind a reversible spectator blanket for ball games or picnics.*

Project: Sporty Spectator Blanket

Perfect for picnics and sporting events, this reversible blanket is warm wool or woolly acrylic on one side and water-proof nylon on the other. Fold it into a handy 15" by 18" carrying pack when not in use. (Fig. 4-30)

Foot: Standard
Stitch: 3-thread
Stitch length: Short
Stitch width: Medium
Thread: Contrasting or matching color
   Needle(s): All-purpose or serger
   Upper looper: Acrylic or cotton crochet
   Lower looper: All-purpose, serger, or woolly nylon
Tension: Tightened lower looper and loosened upper looper
Needle: Size 14/90
Fabric: 1-1/2 yard 60"-wide washable wool or acrylic; 1-1/2 yard 60"-wide waterproof nylon
Notions: 54" of 1"-wide nylon strap-ping; 3/4" *Velcro* square

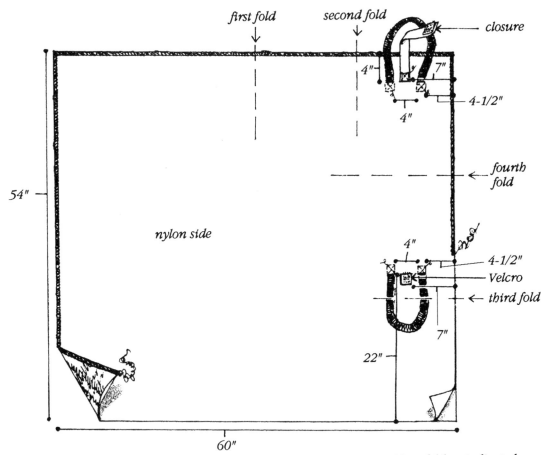

first fold

second fold

closure

4" 7"

4-1/2"

4"

fourth fold

54"

nylon side

4"

4-1/2"

Velcro

third fold

7"

22"

60"

Fig. 4-31: *Top-stitch the closure and straps through both blanket layers. Then fold as indicated, with the nylon side out.*

1. Cut both fabrics exactly 54" by 60".

2. Adjust for a reversible-edge binding stitch.

3. With the wrong sides of the two layers together, serge both lengthwise edges. Then serge the crosswise edges.

4. Secure the thread chain on each corner by threading it back through the binding stitch using a darning needle or a loop turner.

5. Cut 9" of the strapping for the closure and divide the remainder evenly for two straps. Turn under 1/2" on both ends of all three pieces. Straight-stitch one side of the *Velcro* to the closure underside at one end. Straight-stitch the other *Velcro* piece, the opposite closure end, and the strap ends to the nylon side of the blanket at the positions indicated. (Fig. 4-31)

6. Fold the 60" side of the blanket in half, then in half again, keeping the straps and closure on the outside. Fold the blanket in thirds in the other direction, with the closure and straps on top.

Lesson 9.
Reversible
Needle-wrap Stitch

Another decorative reversible stitch is the needle wrap, also called the blanket stitch. In this crochet-like edging, the needle thread wraps to the edge on both sides of the fabric, so the decorative thread used must be threaded through the needle. The looper threads interlock at the edge of the fabric. (Fig. 4-32) Use

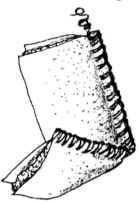

Fig. 4-32: *The reversible needle-wrap stitch makes a crochet-like edging. It is formed when the needle tension is loosened and the looper tension is tightened.*

the needle-wrap stitch as a decorative detail on an already-finished edge (such as a faced neckline or a hem foldline), or use it to finish edges on firmly woven fabric.

Using the standard presser foot, adjust for a short, 3-thread overlock stitch with a medium or narrower stitch width (and the right needle on a 2-needle machine). Loosen the needle tension and tighten the upper and lower looper tensions so the threads interlock on the edge. If the

threads do not overlock exactly at the edge, adjust them with your tweezers.

If you cannot loosen the needle thread entirely to the edge by making a tension adjustment, use a narrower stitch width. Also try monofilament or woolly nylon in the loopers to help perfect this decorative stitch, or remove the needle thread from the tension guides.

The look of a crocheted edge is most easily created by using a long stitch length for the needle-wrap stitch. Using the heaviest possible thread that can fit through the needle eye also looks best.

Project:
Needle-wrap
Needle Case

Use reversible needle-wrap edging on a handy needle case. It keeps a variety of needle sizes at your fingertips and also makes a welcome gift for a sewing friend. (Fig. 4-33)

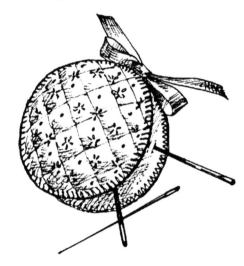

Fig. 4-33: *Quilted fabric, lightweight wool, and a file folder are combined to make a pretty needle case.*

Foot: Standard
Stitch: 3-thread
Stitch length: Medium to long
Stitch width: Medium to narrow (with
    right needle on 2-needle serger)
Thread: Contrasting color
    Needle: Buttonhole twist
    Upper looper: Woolly nylon
    Lower looper: Woolly nylon
Tension: Loosened needle tension
    and tightened looper tensions
Needle: Size 11/75 or 14/90
Fabric: 1/8 yard quilted for outer
    layer; 1/8 yard lightweight woven
    wool for lining
Notions: One file folder; 1/4 yard
    1/4"-wide ribbon

1. Using a lid as a guide, cut two 4-1/2"
circles each from the quilted fabric,
lining, and file folder.

2. Adjust your serger for a reversible
needle-wrap stitch. Test on project
scraps following the previous instructions.

3. Sandwich the file folder circles
between the wrong sides of the outer
fabric and the lining and pin securely.
Because you'll be trimming 1/4" off the
edge as you serge, cut away at least 1" on
the cutting line (see page 33) of both
circles.

4. With the quilted side up, position
your knife on the cutting line in the
trimmed-out section. Serge around the
edge of both circles using the needle-
wrap stitch, trimming 1/4", and keeping
the fabric layer taut. Overlap the beginning stitching for about 1/2". Then raise
the presser foot and needle and pull the
circle away from the foot. Dab the ends
with seam sealant and clip the tails when
dry.

5. After serging, you may have to pull
the needle thread with tweezers so that
the overlocking looper thread is right at
the edge.

6. Place the lining sides of the circles
together and hand-tack for about 1/2" to
join them. Tie the ribbon into a bow and
tack it over the hand-stitching.

5. Decorative Trims, Braids, and Bindings

Decorative trims and bindings can be serged directly onto the edge of your fabric, creating self-binding for craft and home decoration projects as well as for garments from sporty to elegant. Trims and bindings can also be made using a separate strip of fabric that is then attached to your garment or project.

Many of the edge finishes you learned in Chapter 4 can be used separately or in combination to make a wide variety of ornamental trims and bindings. In addition to adding a unique decorative element, trims and bindings also help finish and stabilize project edges.

When applying edge-finishing or self-binding directly to your fabric, always test first for stretching. If the area you will be finishing (especially a bias woven or a cross-grain knit) stretches during the application, serge your trim onto a strip of fabric and bind the edge instead.

Lesson 10. Serged-fold Self-Braid

Many pretty edge finishes are not as stable as we may need for a particular project or fabric. In many cases, a neckline that is finished single-layer will stretch out. Or a single-layer sleeve edge on a loosely woven fabric may not hold up. With serged-fold self-braid, the fabric edge is folded for more durability before serge-finishing. Heavy threads serged on the fold of heavy fabric can look similar to an actual braid trim. Lighter-weight threads serged on the fold of fine fabric give a more delicate, but stable, finish.

1. Press 1/2" to the wrong side. When turning less than a 1/2" allowance, it may be more difficult to keep a uniform edge.

2. Top-stitch 1/8" from the fold with a long stitch length. If your finished project edge will be visible from both sides, trim the allowance close to the top-stitching.

3. Put decorative thread in the upper looper and, if the underside will be visible, also use decorative thread in the lower looper. If only the right side will be exposed, you may use all-purpose or serger thread in the lower looper as well as in the needle.

4. Place the folded edge next to the knife and serge with a short, narrow, balanced, 3-thread stitch. Guide carefully, or use a blindhem foot to prevent cutting the fold (see page 11).

Special Tips: If you are using heavy thread, lengthen the stitch to prevent jamming when you begin to serge. Too much thread coverage may also cause stretching or ruffling of the edge. If your model has differential feed, set it on 1.5 to 2.0 to ease in the edge (especially on bias edges). Always test first on project fabric scraps.

5. If you haven't previously trimmed the excess allowance, do so now. Use sharp embroidery or appliqué scissors and trim close to the serging. (Fig. 5-1)

To vary the serged-fold edge, adjust for a rolled-edge stitch (page 51) or a reversible-edge binding stitch (page 61).

For a more pronounced serged-fold self-braid, serge over filler cord as discussed in Lesson 4 (page 48). (Fig. 5-2) For bias and curved areas, pull on the filler to ease the serged edge.

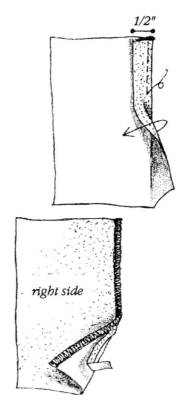

right side

Fig. 5-1: *Create serged-fold self-braid by pressing 1/2" to the wrong side and serge-finishing the fold. Trim the allowance to the stitching before serging if the wrong side will be visible; do this after serging if it will not.*

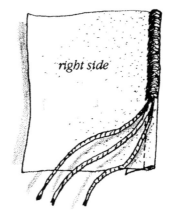

right side

Fig. 5-2: *Serge over filler threads for more pronounced braid.*

Project:
Lacy Hosiery Hangup

Glossy serged-fold self-braid, dainty lace, and luxurious taffeta combine for a practical yet pretty storage solution. (Fig. 5-3)

Fig. 5-3: *Hang a pretty, 12-pocket organizer to keep your hosiery neat and readily available.*

Foot: Standard
Stitch: 3-thread
Stitch length: Short for decorative; medium for serge-finishing
Stitch width: Medium
Thread: Matching or contrasting color
   Needle: All-purpose or serger
   Upper looper: Rayon for decorative; all-purpose or serger for serge-finishing
   Lower looper: All-purpose or serger
Tension: Balanced
Needle: Size 11/75
Fabric: 3/4 yard 45"-wide taffeta for backing; 3/8 yard 45"-wide heavy nylon lace for pockets

Notions: Two 1/4" grommets; 1-1/4 yard 1/4"-wide satin cording or 3/8"-wide ribbon for hanging

1. Cut a 16" by 27" taffeta rectangle for the backing and four 6-1/2" by 20" lace rectangles for pockets.

2. On one short end of the backing fabric, fold 2" to the wrong side, then fold 2" again. Top-stitch to secure.

3. Serge-finish one long edge of each pocket piece.

4. Finish the opposite long edges with serged-fold self-braid, pressing 1/2" to the wrong side and decoratively serging the fold. Trim away the excess fabric on the underside.

5. Position one pocket on the backing with the self-braid 2" below the folded edge and the sides aligned. Fold inverted pleats 5-1/2" from each side, as shown. (Fig. 5-4) Top-stitch the pocket

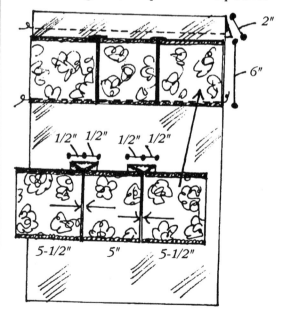

Fig. 5-4: *Fold two inverted pleats in the lace, forming three pockets and aligning the side edges.*

to the backing through the lower, serge-finished edge.

6. Repeat step 5 for the other three pocket rectangles, overlapping the self-braid edges 1" over the serge-finished edge of the previous pocket.

7. To form 12 separate pockets, top-stitch through the centers of the pleats in two vertical rows, 5-1/2" from each side, back-stitching at the top edge of the lace to secure. (Fig. 5-5)

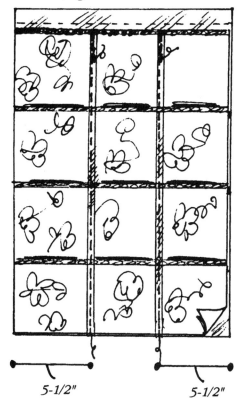

5-1/2"   5-1/2"

Fig. 5-5: *Top-stitch through the pleat centers in two vertical rows.*

8. Finish the sides with serged-fold self-braid, following the previous instructions. Then finish the bottom edge to match.

9. Apply a grommet about 1" from both upper corners. Thread the ends of the cording or ribbon through the grommets from back to front and tie the ends in a bow.

Lesson 11. Quick-fused Self-Braid

Create another simple self-trim by serge-finishing garment or project edges from the wrong side using fusible thread in the lower looper. Then fold the serged edge to the right side and fuse it into position.

The width of the finish can be varied by pressing additional fabric plus the serged edge to the right side. For this variation, the wrong side of the fabric will show as part of the braid. Therefore, the wrong side of the fabric must match or intentionally contrast with the right side.

1. Thread your serger with decorative thread in the upper looper, fusible thread in the lower looper, and all-purpose or serger thread in the needle.

2. From the wrong side, serge-finish the edge with a short, wide, balanced, 3-thread stitch.

3. Press the edge to the right side and fuse it in place. If you are pressing more than the width of the serged stitch to the right side, cut out the project with a corresponding allowance for the extra fabric. (Fig. 5-6)

Fig. 5-6: *For quick-fused self-braid, decoratively finish the edge from the wrong side with fusible thread in the lower looper. Press the stitching to the right side and fuse it next to the edge or further over.*

For a heavier braid, add a wide decorative finish over a narrow self-braid.

1. Serge-finish the edge from the wrong side with a narrow, medium-length, balanced, 3-thread stitch using fusible thread in the lower looper.

2. Fold the stitched edge to the right side and fuse to secure.

3. Change to decorative thread in the lower looper and adjust your serger for a wide satin stitch. Serge over the narrow fused edge. (Fig. 5-7)

Fig. 5-7: *For heavier braid, make a narrow quick-fused self-braid. Then serge over it with decorative thread and a wide stitch.*

Project: Fun Feelies Bag

The casing for this fast and easy bag is decoratively finished with quick-fused self-braid. Little fingers reach into the bag and find matched pairs of fabric squares or buttons by feel alone. (Fig. 5-8)

Fig. 5-8: *Fill a small bag with pairs of distinctively different swatches for an amusing game.*

Foot: Standard
Stitch: 3-thread
Stitch length: Short for decorative; medium for serge-finishing
Stitch width: Widest
Thread: Contrasting color for decorative; matching for serge-finishing
Needle: All-purpose or serger
Upper looper: Crochet thread for decorative; all-purpose or serger for serge-finishing
Lower looper: Fusible thread for decorative; all-purpose or serger for serge-finishing
Tension: Balanced
Needle: Size 11/75
Fabric: 1/4 yard medium-weight cotton or cotton/polyester (or a 7" by 10" scrap)
Notions: One 27" shoelace

1. Cut one 7" by 10" rectangle from the fabric.

2. From the wrong side, decoratively serge-finish one 10" edge for the upper casing (using crochet thread in the upper looper and fusible thread in the lower looper).

3. Rethread the upper and lower loopers with all-purpose or serger thread. Serge-finish the remaining three sides.

4. Fold the bag lengthwise, right sides together, and straight-stitch the lower edge with a 1/4" seam allowance. Pivot at the corner and continue straight-stitching the side seam, ending 1" from the top edge. Back-stitch to secure the stitching. (Fig. 5-9)

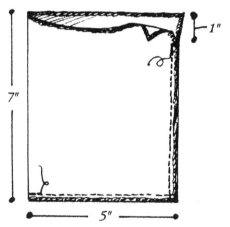

Fig. 5-9: *Straight-stitch the bottom and side of the bag, leaving 1" unstitched at the top edge.*

5. Fold the decoratively serged edge 1" to the right side and carefully press to fuse the casing edge. Top-stitch over the serged needleline to secure. Insert a shoelace into the casing and draw the bag closed.

6. Fill the bag with 12 pairs of distinctly different buttons or 1" fabric squares. Try squares of the plush side of *Velcro*, velvet, grosgrain ribbon, or any other material with a unique texture. A perfect travel game, youngsters try to match as many pairs as possible without peeking.

Lesson 12.
Serged Self-Binding

A simple self-binding technique uses part of the fabric to bind the edge. It is stable as well as decorative and can be a good option for a neckline facing or a center-front band. Self-binding is most often used on straight edges and stable woven fabrics, but it can be applied to curved areas on knit fabrics as well.

The width of the finished binding is determined by the width of the serged stitch. To make a beefy serged self-binding, add a 7/8" binding allowance to the pattern edge and use the widest 3- or 4-thread stitch possible on your serger (usually about 1/4"). Use heavy-weight decorative thread in the upper looper and all-purpose or serger thread in the needle(s) and lower looper.

1. With the wrong side up, serge-finish the edge.

2. Fold the serged edge 7/8" to the wrong side.

3. Rethread the upper looper with all-purpose or serger thread. From the wrong side of the garment, serge along the fold without cutting it. If the width of your stitch is narrower than 1/4", straight-stitch 1/4" from the serged edge. (Fig. 5-10)

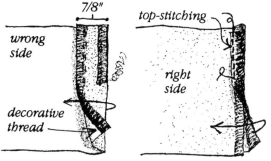

Fig. 5-10: *Fold the decorative edge to the wrong side and serge over the fold. Fold the edge back to the right side and top-stitch.*

4. Fold the decoratively serged edge to the right side (encasing the serged fold). Top-stitch to secure.

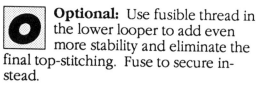 **Optional:** Use fusible thread in the lower looper to add even more stability and eliminate the final top-stitching. Fuse to secure instead.

Project: Canvas Wood Carrier

Serged self-binding stabilizes and decoratively finishes the top of this easy-to-make tote. A 42" length of 45"-wide or wider fabric makes two carriers. (Fig. 5-11)

Foot: Standard
Stitch: 3- or 3/4-thread
Stitch length: Short for decorative; medium for serge-finishing
Stitch width: Widest
Thread: Contrasting color for decorative; matching for serge-finishing

Fig. 5-11: *Make a sturdy wood carrier in a jiffy using serged self-binding, canvas, and webbing.*

Needle(s): All-purpose or serger
Upper looper: Cotton crochet thread for decorative; all-purpose or serger for serging fold and finishing
Lower looper: All-purpose or serger (fusible thread optional)
Tension: Balanced
Needle(s): Size 14/90
Fabric: 1-1/6 yards heavy cotton canvas or cotton duck
Notions: 3 yards 1"-wide cotton webbing

1. Cut a 22" by 42" rectangle from the fabric.

2. Serge-finish the two long edges. Press 1/2" to the wrong side and top-stitch.

3. Apply serged self-braid to the two short ends of the rectangle.

4. Fold 1/2" to the wrong side on both ends of the webbing. Place the straps on the right side of the carrier 5-1/2"

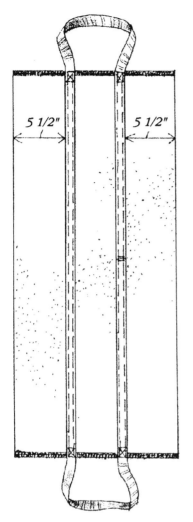

5 1/2"   5 1/2"

Fig. 5-12: *Position the straps on the bag. Top-stitch the edges. Reinforce with square boxes and cross-stitching.*

Lesson 13.
Double-bound Edge

In Lesson 2 (page 39), you learned how to serge a double-bound seam. Fabric is folded over the seam allowances and then decoratively serge-finished. A similar technique is used to create a double-bound edge. Consider using it to trim garment edges or home decorating projects.

A double-bound edge can be serged either directly onto the fabric or onto a binding strip for later application. This edge takes a little more time (just like double-bound seams), but it makes an attractive and durable trim.

1. Cut out the project leaving an extra 1" allowance for all edges that will be double-bound.

2. Fold or press 3/4" to the wrong side on each edge.

3. Adjust for a wide 3- or 3/4-thread stitch and a very short, satin-stitch length. A 7.5mm stitch width will produce a binding more than 1/2" wide (twice the stitch width).

4. With decorative thread in the upper looper and the turned-back fold of the fabric next to the knife, serge on the fold edge with the wrong side of the fabric on top. (Fig. 5-13)

wrong side

Fig. 5-13: *Serge over the fold from the wrong side of the fabric to begin a double-bound edge. Fold the stitching to the right side and top-stitch.*

from each long edge, as shown. (Fig. 5-12) Butt the folded edges together in the middle of the bag piece and top-stitch the webbing on both sides to secure. Reinforce the handles at the top edges of the bag by top-stitching square boxes, then cross-stitch diagonally.

5. Press the serged fold to the right side of the fabric and top-stitch to secure.

 Optional: Use fusible thread in the lower looper, then fuse to secure.

6. Fold the cut edge of the fabric toward the wrong side, forming a fold the exact width of your previous stitching.

7. Serge over the fold with the needleline on top of or right next to the needleline of the previous stitching. (Fig. 5-14)

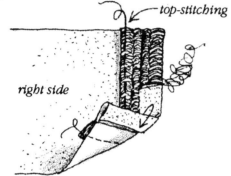

Fig. 5-14: Fold the cut edge toward the wrong side. Serge over the fold, matching needlelines.

8. Trim away any excess allowance close to the stitching on the wrong side of the binding.

Project: Show-off Credit-Card Case

A wide, double-bound edge hides the zipper on this handsome case for credit cards, driver's license, small change, and keys. Tuck it into a pocket when you don't want to carry a purse. (Fig. 5-15)

Foot: Standard
Stitch: 3-thread for decorative; 3- or 3/4-thread for serge-seaming

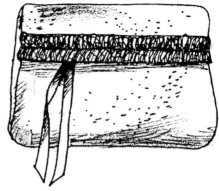

Fig. 5-15: A decorative, double-bound edge ornaments this credit-card case.

Stitch length: Short for decorative; medium for serge-seaming
Stitch width: Widest
Thread: Matching or contrasting color for decorative; matching color for serge-seaming
Needle(s): All-purpose or serger
Upper looper: Pearl rayon or other stable, decorative for double-bound edge; all-purpose or serger for serge-seaming
Lower looper: Fusible, all-purpose, or serger for decorative; all-purpose or serger for serge-seaming
Tension: Balanced
Needle(s): Size 11/75 (or 14/90 for some heavy decorative thread)
Fabric: 1/4 yard *Ultraleather* (or a 5" by 7" scrap)
Notions: One zipper 7" or longer; 6" of 1/4"-wide ribbon

1. Cut a 5" by 7" rectangle from the fabric.

2. Decoratively serge-finish one short end of the rectangle. Center the serge-finished edge on top of the left side of the zipper tape, next to the teeth. (Fig. 5-16)

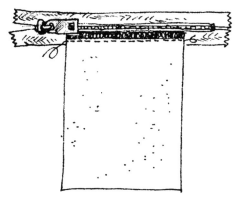

Fig. 5-16: Top-stitch the serge-finished end to one side of the zipper tape.

3. Top-stitch along the needleline of the serging.

4. On the other short end, press 3/4" to the wrong side. With decorative thread in the upper looper, serge-finish the fold from the wrong side. Carefully press the serged fold to the right side and top-stitch next to the overlocked loops. (See the previous instructions for a double-bound edge.)

5. Fold the remaining fabric edge to the wrong side the same width as your previous decorative stitching. Serge over the fold, keeping the needle right on the needleline of the previous stitching.

6. Lap the decorative edge over the unfinished side of the zipper so that the middle of the binding is next to the zipper teeth. With the zipper closed, top-stitch over the previous needleline, securing the decorative edge to the unattached side of the zipper tape. (Fig. 5-17)

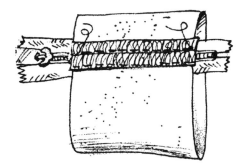

Fig. 5-17: Top-stitch the decorative binding to the right side of the zipper tape.

7. Open the zipper partway and turn the bag inside out. Fold the fabric so the zipper is approximately 1" from the upper edge. Serge-seam the sides of the bag, slowly serging over the zipper tape. (Fig. 5-18)

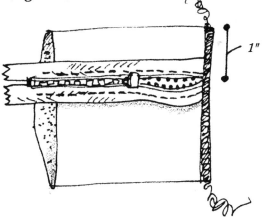

Fig. 5-18: Serge-seam the bag sides from the wrong side.

8. Turn the bag right side out. Knot the ribbon through the zipper pull.

Lesson 14.
Serged Piping

Traditionally, piping is made by tightly covering a cord with fabric, leaving a seam allowance for inserting the piping into a garment or project seam. You can easily replicate traditional piping by serging over filler cord onto a strip of 1-1/4"-wide bias tricot, such as *Seams Great*.

1. Thread the upper looper with decorative thread and adjust for a short, satin-length rolled edge.

2. Serge over one or more strands of heavy thread or cording. Place the filler under the back and over the front of the foot, or use a beading or ribbon foot to help guide it. Refer back to Lesson 4 (page 48) for tips on serging over filler cord.

S **Special Tips:** If your rolled edge is not completely wrapping to the underside, use monofilament or woolly nylon thread in the lower looper. You may need to increase the stitch width if you are serging over several strands of heavy thread or over thick cord. You might also need to increase the stitch length if you have heavy decorative thread in the upper looper.

3. Serge over the filler for several inches, then insert the bias tricot strip under the presser foot. Serge over the strip, trimming about 1/2" with the knives. Do not stretch while serging. At the end, raise the presser foot, and pull the filler tail to the left before chaining off.

4. Insert the piping into a garment or project seam using a straight-stitch and a zipper foot. Or serge the piping into the seam using an optional piping foot, if one is available for your machine.

The filler cord itself may also be used as an ornamental element. Serge over decorative thread, ribbon, or braid using monofilament nylon in the upper looper and a longer stitch length. (Fig. 5-19)

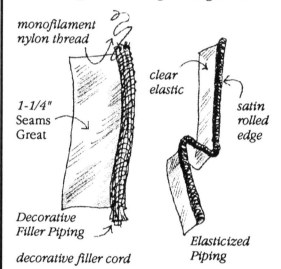

Fig. 5-19: *Serged piping options include featuring the filler cord itself and stretchable piping.*

Elasticized piping

Create a stretchable serged piping for stretch and knit garments by using clear elastic in place of the bias tricot. Stretch the elastic slightly while serge-piping along one edge.

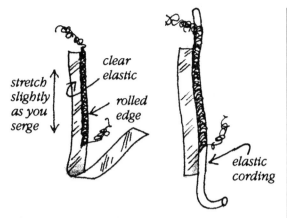

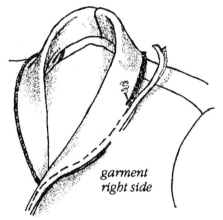

stretch slightly as you serge

clear elastic

rolled edge

elastic cording

Fig. 5-20: *Serge onto clear elastic to make elasticized piping. Add elastic cording under the stitches for a more pronounced effect.*

For maximum coverage, use woolly nylon in the upper looper. (Fig. 5-20)

For more pronounced elasticized piping, serge over a strand of elastic cording as well as the transparent elastic. Thread the elastic cording over the front and under the back of the presser foot (or use a beading or ribbon foot) when serging over the transparent elastic. Be careful not to cut the cording. After making the piping, pull the elastic cording until it lays smoothly.

 Special Tip: When serging over elastic cording, test first—you may need to tighten the upper looper tension so that the thread tightly covers the cording.

Mock piping

Like serged piping, mock piping is made by covering an edge or seamline (with or without filler cord) with a satin rolled edge. It is not considered actual piping, however, because it is serged directly onto the fabric instead of being applied to a bias strip and inserted into a seam. We often see mock piping used as a decorative detail on lightweight robes, pajamas, and casual wear.

To create a simple mock-piped edge, serge along the seamline on the right side of the fabric using a satin rolled edge. Mock piping can be serged single-layer on more stable fabrics or double-layer (wrong sides together). (Fig. 5-21)

garment right side

Fig. 5-21: *Create mock piping by serge-finishing the edges, wrong sides together, with a satin rolled edge.*

On lightweight material, the fabric edge will roll inside the stitching, creating a piped appearance without filler cord. On heavier fabrics, it may not be possible to roll the edge. In this case, loosen the upper looper and adjust for a narrow, satin-length, reversible-edge binding stitch (page 61). Inserting filler cord will add to the piped effect.

A variation of the mock-piped edge is used to create mock-piped bands and cuffs on lightweight fabrics.

1. Fold the band or cuff lengthwise with wrong sides together.

2. Place the band against the wrong side of the fabric, matching the cut edges.

3. Serge mock piping with the band on top. (Fig. 5-22)

Fig. 5-22: For mock piping, place the wrong side of the band against the wrong side of the fabric. Serge-seam with a satin rolled edge.

4. Pull the seam flat and press the allowances away from the band or cuff.

Another mock-piping variation can be used to hem sleeves and lower edges.

1. Lightly press 1/4" to the wrong side. Then press the hem allowance to the wrong side. This technique looks best with a hem allowance of 1" or more. If the hem allowance on your pattern is narrower, add a wider allowance when cutting out the project.

2. Make another fold to the wrong side equal to the hem allowance, sandwiching the 1/4" edge toward the inside of the fold, as shown. (Fig. 5-23)

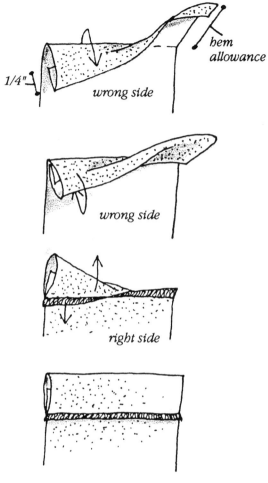

Fig. 5-23: For a mock-piped hem, press 1/4" and then the hem allowance to the wrong side. Fold again and serge with a satin rolled edge. Pull the seam flat.

3. From the right side, serge over the fold with a satin rolled edge, being careful not to cut the fabric.

4. Pull the seam flat and press the allowances away from the folded hem edge. The cut edge will be encased inside the hem.

Elasticized mock piping

Mock piping provides a stable, decorative edge-finish for a neckline or armscye. If the edge needs to stretch with movement, however, such as on swimsuits and exercisewear, use elasticized mock piping instead. (Fig. 5-24)

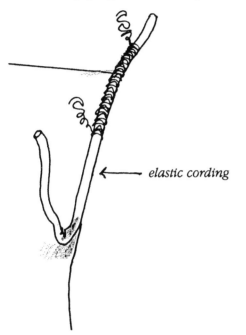

← elastic cording

Fig. 5-24: Finish a stretch-fabric neckline or armscye by serging elasticized piping directly onto the fabric.

To apply elasticized mock piping to a neckline:

1. Trim away the neckline seam allowance. Serge-seam one shoulder.

2. Insert elastic cording under the back and over the front of the presser foot (or use a beading or ribbon foot), and serge a few stitches over the cording. Then place the fabric right side up under the cording and serge the neckline edge. Stretch the cording slightly as you serge.

3. Serge-seam the other shoulder, folding the elastic cording back toward the garment and serging over it as you complete the seam. (Fig. 5-25) Be

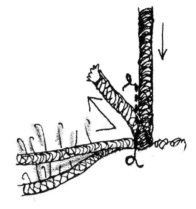

Fig. 5-25: Serge the remaining seam, folding the cording back. Straight-stitch over the needleline to secure before trimming the tail.

careful not to cut the cording. Straight-stitch over the cording to secure it before trimming the end.

N Note: Apply elasticized mock piping to an armscye following the neckline procedure above, with one exception: instead of serging two shoulder seams, serge the shoulder seam first, then the side seam.

Project: Serge-piped Eyeglass Case

Serged piping accents the upper edge of this simple-to-serge accessory. As well as carrying your glasses in style, the case also makes a great gift or bazaar item. (Fig. 5-26)

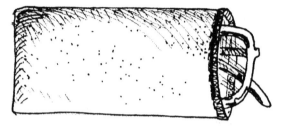

Fig. 5-26: *Use Ultrasuede or Ultraleather scraps for a fashionable eyeglass case.*

Foot: Beading, ribbon, or standard for piping and trim; standard for serge-seaming
Stitch: 3-thread for rolled-edge piping and trim; 3- or 3/4-thread for serge-seaming
Stitch length: Short for piping and trim; medium for serge-seaming
Stitch width: Narrow for piping and trim; medium or wider for serge-seaming
Thread: Contrasting color
    Needle(s): All-purpose or serger
    Upper looper: #8 pearl cotton for piping; all-purpose or serger for serge-seaming
    Lower looper: Monofilament nylon for piping; all-purpose or serger for serge-seaming
Filler: 4 strands of #5 pearl cotton, the same color as the upper looper thread
Tension: Rolled edge for piping; balanced for serge-seaming
Needle(s): Size 14/90

Fabric: 1/4 yard *Ultrasuede* or *Ultraleather* (or a 7" by 8" scrap)
Notions: 1 yard 1-1/4" *Seams Great*

1. Cut a 7" by 8" rectangle from the fabric.

2. With a satin-length, rolled-edge stitch and decorative thread in the upper looper, serge over the four strands of #5 pearl cotton onto the *Seams Great* to make at least 16" of serged piping.

3. For the upper edge, center the best 9" section of serged piping on the right side of one 7" side. Using a zipper foot, straight-stitch next to the piping. You will have 1" tails of piping extending past the edge. (Fig. 5-27)

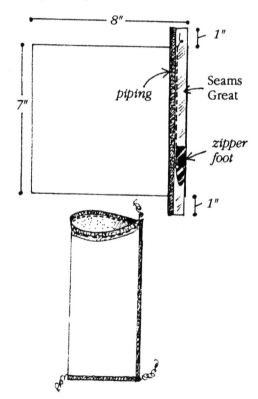

Fig. 5-27: *Straight-stitch the piping to the fabric. After turning the piping to the edge, top-stitching, and trimming, serge-seam the unfinished edges.*

4. Turn the Seams Great to the underside of the fabric, positioning the piping on the edge. Top-stitch through both layers next to the piping. Trim away the excess Seams Great next to the top-stitching.

5. Fold the case right sides together and serge-seam the lower edge and side. Secure the ends with seam sealant and clip the tails when dry, then turn the case right side out.

Lesson 15.
Serged Binding

Finding just the right decorative trim for your garment or project often can be difficult. Now you have a wide range of options for designing and serging your own. The base fabric width, content, and color can be varied. And you can use a large assortment of thread types and colors. Any decorative edging stitch is a possibility. Always test first.

1. Select a bias strip of woven fabric or a cross-grain strip of knit that matches or contrasts with the fabric you are binding. Cut the length you'll need plus 1". The width of the bias strip should measure your desired finished trim width plus 1/2". For a 3/4"-wide trim, you'll need a strip 1-1/4" wide.

2. On one long edge, press 1/4" to the wrong side.

3. Adjust your serger for a balanced, 3-thread stitch or any other decorative stitch you would like on your trim.

4. With decorative thread in the upper looper and the fold next to the knife, serge carefully along the fold without cutting the fabric. Use a blindhem foot, if available, for accurate guiding.

 Special Tip: For the easiest finishing, use fusible thread in the lower looper and a medium to wide, balanced stitch.

5. Place the decorative side of the strip against the wrong side of the project fabric, aligning the cut edges.

6. Using all-purpose or serger thread, serge the edge with a 1/4" seam. If your stitch is not that wide, serge-seam first, then straight-stitch at the 1/4" seamline. (Fig. 5-28)

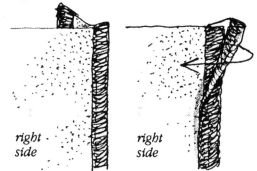

right side

right side

Fig. 5-28: *Decoratively serge the binding strip. Serge-seam the strip to the fabric, then wrap the decorative serging to the right side and fuse or top-stitch.*

7. Wrap the trim to the right side, encasing the seam.

8. Carefully press the trim in place and top-stitch to secure. If you've used fusible thread, carefully fuse the trim in place. Then top-stitching is optional, but it will add durability.

9. To add more texture or color to your trim, you may choose to use a wider binding and decoratively serge over the folded edge (without cutting it). Use a different stitch or stitch width for variety. (Fig. 5-29)

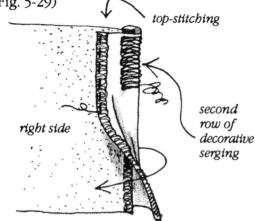

Fig. 5-29: *Add more color and texture to serged binding with a wider strip. Then decoratively serge again after folding and securing the binding on the right side.*

Project: Handy Hanging Hamper

Collect your laundry in style inside an attractive hamper trimmed with serged binding. (Fig. 5-30)

Foot: Standard
Stitch: 3-thread for decorative; 3- or 3/4-thread for serge-seaming
Stitch length: Short for decorative; medium for serge-seaming
Stitch width: Widest
Thread: Contrasting color
  Needle(s): All-purpose or serger
  Upper looper: Crochet for decorative; all-purpose or serger for serge-seaming
  Lower looper: All-purpose, serger, or fusible for decorative; all-purpose or serger for serge-seaming

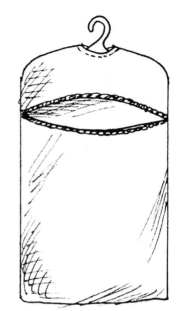

Fig. 5-30: *Hang a serge-bound laundry hamper in your closet or on the back of a door.*

Tension: Balanced
Needle(s): Size 14/90
Fabric: 1 yard cotton canvas, cotton duck, or heavy nylon

1. Make the hamper back pattern by tracing around a plastic hanger at the top. Then extend the pattern 1/2" on both sides and 36" in length. Add 1/2" seam allowances to all sides. Curve out the top for the hanger opening. (Fig. 5-31)

2. For the front pattern, trace the back and draw a front opening, as shown, separating the pattern into two pieces.

3. Using the patterns, cut out all three hamper pieces.

4. Cut 1-1/4"-wide bias strips from the remaining fabric (piece if necessary). You'll need enough to trim both opening edges plus 2". On one long edge of the strip, carefully press 1/4" to the wrong side.

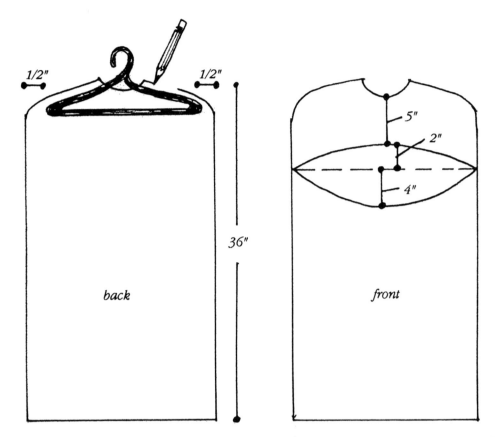

Fig. 5-31: *For the pattern back, trace around the top of a hanger. Add 1/2" at each side and extend the sides 36". For the front, trace the back and draw the hamper opening.*

5. Adjust your serger for a short, wide, balanced stitch and decoratively serge the folded edge.

6. Along one side of the hamper opening, serge-seam the cut edge of the right side of the trim to the wrong side of the fabric. If your serger does not have a 1/4" stitch width, straight-stitch on the 1/4" seamline after serge-seaming. Wrap the binding to the right side and top-stitch. (Fig. 5-32)

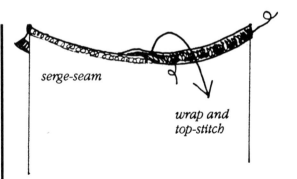

Fig. 5-32: *Apply serged binding to the curved opening edges.*

Optional: Use fusible thread in the lower looper of the decorative stitching and fuse instead of top-stitching.

7. Repeat step 6 for the opposite opening edge.

8. Change to all-purpose or serger thread in the loopers, and serge-finish the hanger opening edges. Turn 3/8" to the wrong side and top-stitch.

9. Place the right sides of the front and back hamper pieces together, with the serge-bound edges overlapping 1/2". (Fig. 5-33) Because of the overlapping,

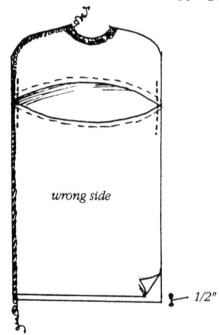

wrong side

— 1/2"

Fig. 5-33: *Place the hamper front and back right sides together for serge-seaming. Trim off the extra 1/2" on the bottom of the back as you serge-seam.*

the back will be 1/2" longer than the front.

10. Serge-seam the sides and lower edge, trimming off the extra 1/2" on the back. Secure the lapped binding ends by straight-stitching along the seamline using a short stitch length. Turn right side out.

Lesson 16.
Serge-piped Binding

A popular variation of the serged piping in Lesson 14 is constructed with a narrow rolled edge and a satin-stitch length. This binding gives the appearance of piping without having to go through the extra steps of inserting a piping strip. Serge-piped binding makes a pretty, delicate finish on lightweight or silky fabric—great for neckline and sleeve edges.

1. Cut a bias strip of woven fabric or a cross-grain strip of knit for the binding. Cut the length you'll need plus 1". The width of the bias strip should measure your desired finished trim width plus 3/4". For a 1/2"-wide finished binding, cut the binding strips 1-1/4" wide.

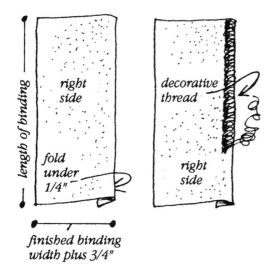

length of binding

right side

fold under 1/4"

decorative thread

right side

finished binding width plus 3/4"

Fig. 5-34: *Make serge-piped binding by pressing 1/4" to the wrong side and serging a rolled edge on the fold.*

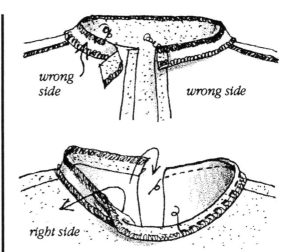

wrong side

wrong side

right side

Fig. 5-35: *Serge the binding to the wrong side of the edge. Wrap it to the right side and straight-stitch along the rolled-edge needleline.*

2. On one long edge, press 1/4" to the wrong side. (Fig. 5-34)

3. Serge-finish the fold with a narrow rolled edge adjusted to a short, satin-stitch length. Use decorative thread in the upper looper and matching all-purpose or serger thread in the needle and lower looper. Shiny rayon thread is a good choice for silky fabric because it complements the fabric texture.

4. Place the right side of the binding on the wrong side of the project fabric with cut edges matching.

5. Serge a 1/4" seam. (Fig. 5-35) If your widest serged stitch is narrower than 1/4", straight-stitch at the 1/4" seamline after serge-seaming.

6. Fold the binding to the right side and straight-stitch on top of the rolled-edge needleline. Use a zipper foot to help position your stitches accurately.

Project: Microwave Roll Warmer

Serge-piped binding finishes the oval edge of this quilted roll warmer. Enlarge the measurements for a larger warmer. (Fig. 5-36)

Fig. 5-36: *Use serge-piped binding to decorate this practical roll warmer. It keeps bread moist and fresh from the microwave to the table.*

Foot: Rolled edge or standard for decorative (depending on model); standard for serge-seaming

Stitch: Rolled edge for decorative; 3-thread for serge-seaming

Stitch length: Satin for decorative; medium for serge-seaming

Stitch width: Narrow for decorative; wide for serge-seaming

Thread: Contrasting color for decorative; matching for serge-seaming

Needle: All-purpose or serger

Upper looper: #8 pearl cotton for decorative; all-purpose or serger for serge-seaming

Lower looper: Woolly nylon for decorative; all-purpose or serger for serge-seaming

Tension: Rolled edge for decorative; balanced for serge-seaming

Needle: Size 14/90

Fabric: 1/3 yard 45"-wide double-sided, quilted cotton; 1-1/4 yard matching or contrasting 1-1/4"-wide bias binding

1. From the fabric, cut two 8" by 10" rectangles. Round the corners using a saucer as a guide.

2. For the binding, press 1/4" to the wrong side along one long edge of the bias strip. With decorative thread in the upper looper, serge-finish over the fold with a rolled-edge stitch.

3. Serge-seam the binding to half of one oval, as shown. (Fig. 5-37) Place the right side of the binding on the wrong side of the fabric, matching the cut edges.

4. Wrap the binding around the seam allowance to the right side, but do not fold the seam allowance. Straight-stitch on the rolled-edge needleline to secure.

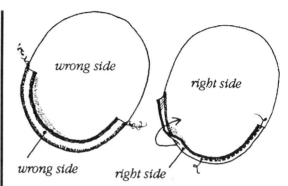

Fig. 5-37: Serge-seam the binding to the warmer top, wrap it to the right side, and top-stitch it in place.

5. Place the two ovals wrong sides together. At 1/3 the oval length, pin the finished flap toward the center, as shown. (Fig. 5-38) Beginning at the opposite end, place the right side of the

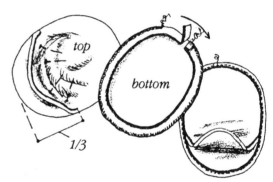

Fig. 5-38: Pin the bound edge of the top toward the center. From the bottom of the warmer, serge-seam the binding around the entire edge. Turn and top-stitch the binding to the top side.

binding strip against the underside of the warmer, with 1/2" of the strip folded back on itself. Serge-seam the binding to the warmer, covering all the unfinished edges. Lap the end of the strip over the beginning fold to complete the seam.

6. Fold the binding evenly around the allowance to the right side. Straight-stitch on the rolled-edge needleline to secure.

Lesson 17. Double Rolled-edge Braid and Binding

The double rolled edge featured in Lesson 5 (page 53) can be adapted to make both a narrow braid and a decorative binding. Using contrasting thread colors for the two rolled edges accents the delicate technique. Because maximum thread coverage and a perfectly rolled edge are important, we often choose woolly nylon for both the upper and lower loopers.

Double rolled-edge braid

To make double rolled-edge braid for trimming your garments, home decorations, or craft projects, serge over a 1/2"-wide strip of base fabric. Choose any lightweight fabric that matches or blends with the upper looper thread color.

1. Adjust your serger for a satin rolled edge.

2. Serge one long edge of the fabric strip, leaving a thread chain several inches long.

3. Rethread the upper looper with a contrasting-color thread. Serge the other side of the strip with the needle on, or right next to, the needleline of the origi-

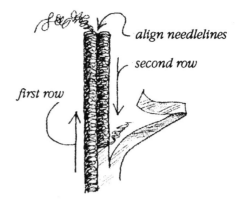

Fig. 5-39: Make a double rolled-edge braid trim by serging two rows of rolled edging on a fabric strip, aligning the needlelines.

nal serging. (Fig. 5-39) Hold the thread chain taut to start the serging without jamming. Aligning the needlelines accurately and perfecting this technique may take a little practice.

4. Top-stitch the braid to your project fabric, stitching directly on the center needleline.

Double rolled-edge binding

Make a matching decorative binding by serge-finishing the folded edge of a bias-woven or a cross-grain knit binding strip, using a double rolled-edge technique. Choose a lightweight fabric that matches or blends with the thread colors and the fabric to be bound.

1. Cut and piece the binding strip twice your finished binding width plus 1-1/2" by the length you'll need for your project. Fold the strip in half lengthwise with wrong sides together.

2. Serge the fold with a satin rolled edge. From the wrong side, press the binding open.

3. Rethread the upper looper with a contrasting-color thread. Then refold the binding strip and serge-finish the edge with the needlelines on top of, or right next to, each other. (Fig. 5-40)

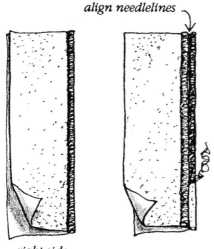

align needlelines

right side

Fig. 5-40: *For double rolled-edge binding, serge-finish a fold. Then refold and serge an adjoining rolled edge.*

⬤ **Optional:** For a wider trim, cut the strip wider and serge three or more rows. Allow about 3/8" of fabric for each additional rolled-edge row.

4. Place the right side of the binding against the wrong side of the fabric, matching the cut edges. Serge-seam with your widest stitch, or straight-stitch a 1/4" seam. If you are applying the binding to an outside curve, ease the binding around the curve.

5. Press the binding to the right side and top-stitch between the rolled-edge rows to secure. (Fig. 5-41)

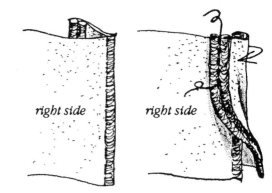

right side   *right side*

Fig. 5-41: *Serge-seam double rolled-edge binding to the fabric edge. Wrap it to the right side and top-stitch on the center needleline.*

Project: Armchair Sewing Caddy

Double rolled-edge binding finishes the pockets and edges of this handy sewing caddy. All of your supplies are at your fingertips while you visit or watch TV. (Fig. 5-42)

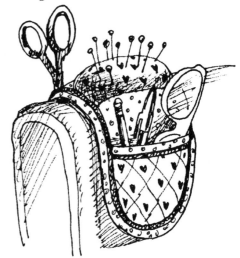

Fig. 5-42: *This simple sewing caddy is a thoughtful gift for your favorite seamstress or crafter.*

Foot: Rolled edge or standard for decorative (depending on model); standard for serge-seaming

Stitch: Rolled edge for decorative; 3- or 3/4-thread for serge-seaming

Stitch length: Short for decorative; medium for serge-seaming

Stitch width: Narrow for decorative; widest for serge-seaming

Thread: Contrasting colors

    Needle(s): All-purpose or serger

    Upper looper: Two contrasting colors of woolly nylon for decorative; all-purpose or serger for serge-seaming

    Lower looper: Woolly nylon for decorative; all-purpose or serger for serge-seaming

Tension: Rolled edge for decorative; balanced for serge-seaming

Needle(s): Size 11/75

Fabric: 1/6 yard 45"-wide double-sided quilted; 2-1/2" by 60" matching or contrasting bias strip

Notions: Approximately one handful of polyester fiberfill

1. Cut one 4-1/2" by 16" rectangle for the caddy, two 4-1/2" by 4" rectangles for the pockets, and one 4-1/2" by 5" rectangle for the pincushion. Place the pockets over the caddy ends, matching the cut edges. Using a saucer or cup, round all four corners. (Fig. 5-43)

2. Make double rolled-edge binding on the bias strip following the previous instructions. Trim the strip width to 1".

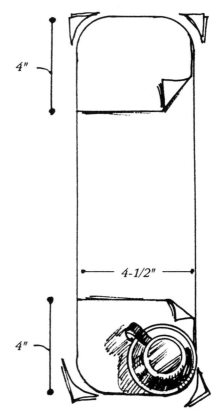

Fig. 5-43: *Position the pockets over the caddy ends and round all four corners.*

3. Bind the upper (straight) edge of the pockets by applying the right side of the binding to the wrong side of the pocket. Wrap the binding to the right side and top-stitch on the rolled-edge needleline.

4. With the wrong side of the two long edges together, serge-seam the pincushion, leaving the ends open. Lightly stuff with fiberfill. Pin the pincushion across

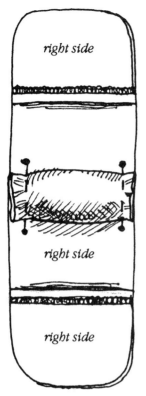

right side

right side

right side

Fig. 5-44: *Place the pincushion and pockets on the right side before serge-seaming the binding from the underside.*

the center of the caddy with the seam allowance underneath. (Fig. 5-44)

5. Place the wrong side of the pocket pieces on the right side of the caddy, matching the cut edges.

6. On one short end, fold the binding strip 1/2" to the wrong side. Beginning in the middle of one end, place the right side of the folded end of the binding against the back side of the caddy, matching the cut edges (see Fig. 5-38). Serge with a 1/4" seam allowance, lapping the end of the strip over the beginning fold as you complete the seam and being careful not to hit the pins. If your

serger does not have a stitch as wide as 1/4", straight-stitch on the 1/4" seamline after serging.

7. Fold the binding to the right side and top-stitch on the rolled-edge needleline to secure.

Lesson 18. Elasticized Trims and Binding

The serger makes sewing stretch and knit fabrics a breeze. Now you can also serge elasticized trims and binding to add decorative detail and to individualize your garments.

Elasticized Trims

A classic example of new products leading to new techniques, serging elasticized trim was never an option before the introduction of clear elastic. Now we can make a variety of stretch trims to coordinate with any stretch or knit fabric. Using different stitch widths, tension adjustments, and thread types adds to the possibilities.

Because clear elastic is so lightweight, it is important to serge through it to keep it from rolling. Neatly trim any excess elastic after serging the trim. If available, use an elastic foot to accurately guide narrow elastic. Loosen the foot's tension to prevent the elastic from stretching as it is serged over.

Single-stretch trim
1. Begin with a single row of serging on a piece of clear elastic. Test various widths.

2. Adjust the stitch width to the width of braid desired. The elastic width must be wider than the stitch width.

3. Serge, using a short (not satin), 2mm stitch length. For better coverage, use woolly nylon in both loopers.

4. Adjust the tension for a balanced, 3-thread stitch, making it loose enough to allow the elastic to lie flat. After serging several inches, test the braid by stretching. If the stitches break, loosen the needle thread tension or stretch the elastic slightly as you serge.

5. If you're not using an elastic foot, hold the elastic taut in front of and behind the presser foot while serging. It is not necessary to stretch the elastic because the serged stitch allows for stretch.

6. Trim the elastic close to the serging, being careful not to cut the stitches. (Fig. 5-45) If part of the elastic still remains, it won't show after the trim is top-stitched to the garment.

7. Top-stitch the trim to the garment using a long straight-stitch or a very narrow zigzag and sewing close to each edge of the trim. Stretch the elastic as you sew.

Double-stretch trim

Select an elastic that is wider than the trim you will be making.

1. Serge one side of the elastic following the previous guidelines, but do not trim the elastic.

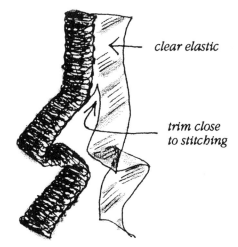

clear elastic

trim close to stitching

Fig. 5-45: Decoratively serge clear elastic, then trim it close to the stitching to make single-stretch trim.

2. On the opposite (unserged) side, serge another row with the needle just inside or next to the needleline of the previous stitching. (Fig. 5-46) For variation, use a different thread color in the upper looper when serging the second side.

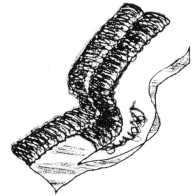

Fig. 5-46: Double-stretch trim features a second row of serging with needlelines aligned.

3. Top-stitch the trim to the garment using a long stitch and sewing close to each edge of the trim. Stretch the elastic as you sew.

Stretch-trim variations

Adjust your serger for a narrow, balanced stitch. Tighten the lower looper tension slightly. Serge the elastic, following the directions for the double-stretch trim.

Try serging a balanced stitch on one side and a rolled-edge stitch on the other side. Or serge a rolled edge on both sides, overlapping the needlelines. (Fig. 5-47) For more elasticity when serging a

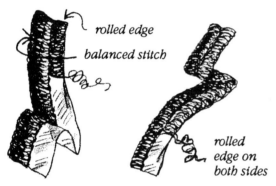

rolled edge

balanced stitch

rolled edge on both sides

Fig. 5-47: Stretch-trim variations include double trim with one or two rolled edges.

rolled edge on clear elastic, stretch the elastic. It will return to its original length after serging.

Braided trim

Braid the elastic trim for swimsuit or camisole straps:

1. Serge a strand of single-stretch trim six times the length of the strap plus 6".

Fig. 5-48: Braided stretch trim is used for swimsuit and camisole straps.

2. Cut the trim into six equal lengths. Braid it into two straps and secure the ends with straight-stitching. (Fig. 5-48)

3. Attach the straps to your garment according to the pattern guidesheet.

Elasticized Binding

Elasticized binding adds stretch and stability to an edge and is neat and decorative at the same time. You have the option of leaving one serged-finished edge exposed on the underside of the binding or wrapping and twin-needle top-stitching to leave no serged edges exposed.

Elasticized binding works especially well on stretch fabrics because the serged stitch used to apply the elastic is a stretch stitch. Use it to finish the edges of swimsuits or exercisewear. You can even extend the binding past the garment edge to form straps.

Any width elastic can be used, but 3/8" is the most versatile. Select any type except clear elastic (it will roll inside the binding).

To bind the edge of stretch fabric:

1. Cut the elastic to the desired length. Cut a stretch binding strip the same length. Its width should be three times the width of the elastic plus 1/4". For a heavy or thick fabric, cut the strip an additional 1/4" wider.

2. Serge-finish one long edge of the strip using a medium-width, medium-length, 3-thread stitch, trimming only slightly to neaten.

3. Place the right sides of the binding and fabric together, matching the cut edges. Straight-stitch with a seam allowance the width of the elastic (usually 3/8"). Stretch the layers as you sew. (Fig. 5-49)

4. Adjust the serger for a long, balanced, 3-thread stitch. Place the elastic on top of the binding, next to the edge. Serge it to the seam allowance through all layers.

5. Fold the binding to the wrong side, encasing the serged seam allowance. From the right side, top-stitch on the binding with a narrow zigzag or a twin needle to secure, stretching slightly as you sew. Or stitch-in-the-ditch from the right side, stretching firmly. (Fig. 5-50)

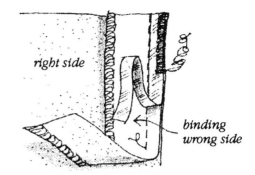

Fig. 5-49: *For elasticized binding, straight-stitch the binding to the garment, stretching both layers. Serge elastic to the seam allowance on top of the binding.*

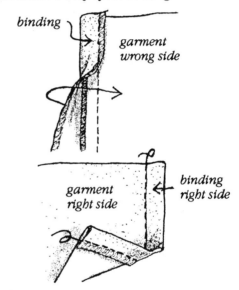

Fig. 5-50: *Fold the binding to the wrong side and top-stitch or stitch-in-the-ditch.*

O **Optional:** To make a binding with no exposed serging, the width of the binding strip should be four times the width of the elastic plus 1/4". Don't serge-finish one long edge. After applying (steps 3 and 4), fold the unsewn edge of the binding 3/8" (the width of the seam allowance) to the wrong side, matching the cut edge to the serged edge. Fold 3/8" again, encasing the serged elastic. From the right side, top-stitch as in step 5. (Fig. 5-51)

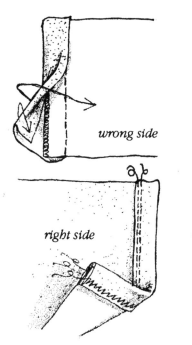

wrong side

right side

Fig. 5-51: *For elasticized binding with no exposed serging, fold the unsewn edge to the wrong side and wrap it to encase the elastic. Top-stitch or stitch-in-the-ditch to secure.*

The application of elasticized binding varies slightly from stretch fabrics to wovens. When elasticized binding is applied to the edge of woven fabric, the fabric is gathered in with the elastic, so the fabric and binding must be cut larger than the opening.

1. Cut the elastic smaller than the opening, to the desired length.

2. If you are applying the binding to a curved area, cut the trim strip on the bias to allow it to lie smoothly.

3. Straight-stitch the binding to the fabric without stretching.

4. When applying the elastic, stretch the elastic to fit the length of the binding as you serge.

5. Finish as instructed for the stretch binding.

Project: Terry-Towel Wrap

Elasticized binding anchors this thirsty wrap. Use it by the pool, after a bath or gym class, or at the spa. (Fig. 5-52)

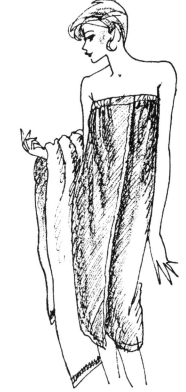

Fig. 5-52: *Wrap up in comfortable terry featuring elasticized binding.*

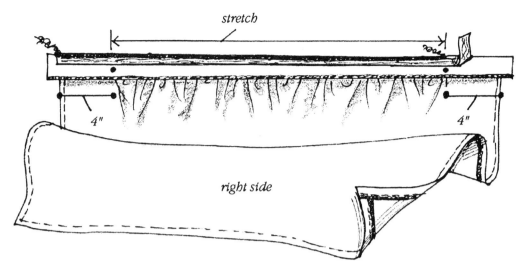

stretch

4"   4"

right side

Fig. 5-53: *Serge-seam the elastic to the binding edge, stretching between the 4" markings.*

Foot: Standard
Stitch: 3-thread
Stitch length: Medium for serge-
   finishing; long for serge-seaming
   elastic
Stitch width: Widest
Thread: Matching color
   Needle: All-purpose or serger
   Upper looper: All-purpose or serger
   Lower looper: All-purpose or serger
Tension: Balanced
Needle: Size 11/75
Fabric: 1-1/3 yard 60"-wide terry; one
   binding strip 2-3/4" wide by 60"
   long from nylon/*Lycra* or contrast-
   ing fabric
Notions: 3/4"-wide elastic the length of
   the bust measurement plus 6"; 4" of
   3/4"-wide *Velcro*

1. Serge-finish one long edge (for the lower edge) and both short edges. Turn 3/4" to the wrong side on the long edge and top-stitch to hem. Repeat for the short (side) edges.

2. Serge-finish one long edge of the binding strip, trimming slightly.

3. With 3/4" extending on each end, place the binding strip and the upper edge right sides together. Straight-stitch with a 3/4" seam allowance.

4. Place the elastic snugly around the upper bust, overlapping it 4". Cut to that length.

5. Mark the binding 4" from each edge of the fabric. With a long stitch length, serge-seam the elastic to the binding and fabric, stretching it to fit between the markings. (Fig. 5-53)

6. Turn the 3/4" ends to the wrong side and fold the binding to the wrong side, encasing the ends, elastic, and serged seam allowance. From the right side, stitch-in-the-ditch to secure.

7. Top-stitch the hooked side of the *Velcro* to the under layer of the wrap and the looped section to the underside of the top layer, as shown. (Fig. 5-54)

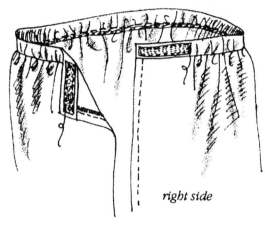

right side

Fig. 5-54: *Straight-stitch the* Velcro *to the binding to fasten the wrap.*

Lesson 19.
Tear-away Braid

Make a simple, balanced braid by serging over tear-away stabilizer using decorative thread (such as pearl cotton) and a satin-stitch length. Serge-decorate one or both edges of the braid or join several widths together using a narrow zigzag.

1. Adjust for a wide, satin-length, balanced, 3-thread stitch using pearl cotton or another heavy decorative thread in the loopers and all-purpose or serger thread in the needle. (To prevent jamming, remember to begin with a medium stitch length and shorten it as needed to perfect the satin stitch.)

2. Serge over a strip of tear-away stabilizer the length of braid you'll need. (Fig. 5-55) You may need to lap the short ends of several stabilizer strips.

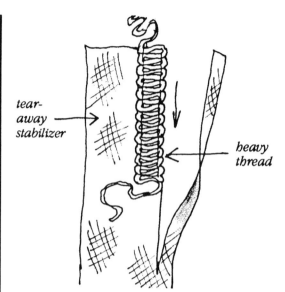

tear-away stabilizer

heavy thread

Fig. 5-55: *Serge a chunky braid over tear-away stabilizer.*

3. Straight-stitch over both long edges and tear away the stabilizer.

Make a braid of any width by placing two or more braid strands side by side and joining them with a zigzag stitch. Use matching or monofilament nylon thread in the needle of a narrow zigzag for nearly invisible seaming, or use a contrasting color and a wider zigzag for a decorative effect. (Fig. 5-56) For a

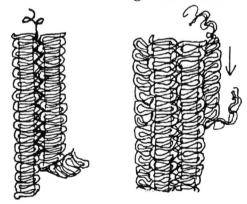

Fig. 5-56: *Zigzag together two or more rows of tear-away braid. Edge with serged-on picots, if desired.*

decorative edge on either single- or multiple-width tear-away braid, serge one or both edges from the wrong side with a picot-braid edge (see page 49).

O **Optional:** For fusible tear-away braid, use fusible thread in the lower looper, adjusting so that the decorative thread just wraps the edge and the fusible thread is not visible from the right side of the braid. Or, use fusible thread in the bobbin when straight-stitching the braid edges and, for multiple strands, also use fusible thread in the bobbin of the zigzag stitch. Fuse the braid to the fabric, using a press cloth. If desired, top-stitch for added durability.

Project: Elegant Bedside Caddy

Lace and tear-away braid team up to decorate a functional yet pretty bedside organizer. A tuck-under panel slips beneath the mattress to hold the caddy firmly in place. (Fig. 5-57)

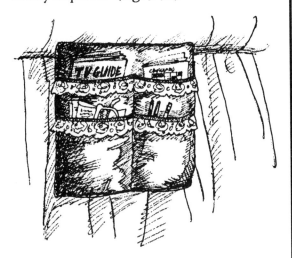

Fig. 5-57: End night-table clutter with a feminine bedside caddy.

Foot: Standard
Stitch: 3-thread
Stitch length: Short for braid; medium for serge-seaming
Stitch width: Widest
Thread: Contrasting color for braid; matching for serge-seaming
  Needle: All-purpose or serger
  Upper looper: Heavy rayon for braid; all-purpose or serger for serge-seaming
  Lower looper: All-purpose or serger
Tension: Balanced
Needle: Size 14/90
Fabric: 1 yard taffeta
Notions: 3/4 yard 1-1/4"-wide flat lace edging; 3/8 yard heavy fusible interfacing; 4" by 36" strip tear-away stabilizer

1. From the taffeta, cut two 12" by 13" rectangles for the caddy, one 12" by 20" rectangle and one 12" by 14" rectangle for the pockets, and one 12" by 23-1/4" rectangle for the tuck-under. Also cut a 12" by 13" rectangle of the interfacing.

2. Fuse the interfacing to the wrong side of one of the 12" by 13" rectangles. Press both pockets in half, wrong sides together, with the short ends aligned (these ends will be at the bottom edge of the caddy).

3. Top-stitch lace along the folded edge of both pockets.

4. Serge 36" of tear-away braid over the stabilizer, following the previous instructions.

5. Cut two 12" strands of braid and top-stitch it to the upper edge of each pocket, over the lace edge. (Fig. 5-58)

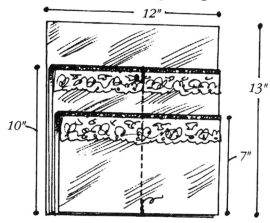

Fig. 5-58: *Top-stitch the braid over the folded pocket edges before positioning them on the caddy and straight-stitching down the center.*

6. Position both pockets on the inter-faced caddy as shown, matching the lower cut edges.

7. Straight-stitch down the center of both pockets, dividing each into two sections and attaching them to the caddy.

8. Place the second caddy rectangle right sides together with the caddy front. Serge-seam the lower edge and sides, catching the pockets in the stitching. Using a short stitch length, straight-stitch over the braid ends on the serging needleline. Turn the caddy right side out and press carefully.

9. Fold the short ends of the tuck-under rectangle right sides together and serge-seam. Also serge-seam one other open end. Turn right side out and press.

10. Position the tuck-under on the right side of the caddy with the unfinished edges matching. Serge-seam the caddy to the tuck-under. Press the seam allowance toward the tuck-under and top-stitch.

Lesson 20. Puffed Serged Braid

A thread chain serged from heavy decorative thread can be used as ornamental braid. Serging over several strands of filler (as described in previous lessons) makes a heavier braid. For an even chunkier, puffed braid, serge over rolled fabric or thick yarn.

A strip of 1"-wide tricot, interlock, or jersey (cut on the crosswise grain) can be used for the puff-braid filler. Or use 5/8"-wide Seams Great for a more deli-cate braid. When pulled, the fabric strip rolls into a narrow tube and serged stitches can be formed around it. The resulting puffed braid is ideal for edging, couching, and craft projects.

Use decorative thread in the upper and lower loopers with matching all-purpose or serger thread in the needle. Use heavier decorative thread when serging over thicker fabric such as jersey; use finer thread for serging over lightweight filler.

For a heavier braid, remove the presser foot or use a beading foot. For a thinner braid, you may be able to use the standard presser foot. Test for the best results.

1. Adjust for a wide, medium-length, balanced stitch with the lower looper slightly tightened.

2. Pull the fabric strip slightly so that it

rolls into a tube. Place the tube between the needle and the knife. If you are using a presser foot, put the tube under the back and over the front of the foot (or use a beading foot). Allow approximately 1" of the tube to extend in back of the foot.

3. Hold the end of the tube taut behind the foot to prevent jamming as you begin to serge. If you are not using a foot, carefully guide the taut tube between the needle and knife.

4. Continue to hold the serged braid taut (but don't pull), guiding it smoothly out behind the foot or needle. The stitches should form around, and not through, the tube. (Fig. 5-59)

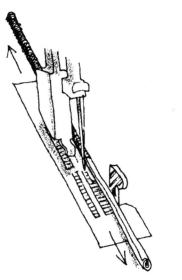

Fig. 5-59: *Make puffed serged braid by serging around a fabric tube or chunky yarn.*

Puffed serged braid may be hand-tacked to your fabric to form a letter or design. Twist or braid strands together for a more pronounced trim. (Fig. 5-60)

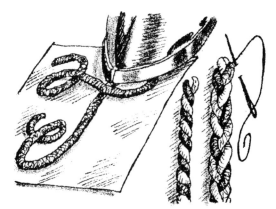

Fig. 5-60: *Puffed serged braid can be tacked or fused to fabric to form letters or designs. Twist or braid multiple strands for a pronounced effect.*

S **Special Tip:** Use fusible thread in the lower looper to create fusible puffed braid. In most instances, the fusible thread will permanently bond the braid in place. For more durability, hand-tack the braid to the fabric, catching only the under side of the braid.

Frog Closures

Make traditional frog closures by serging over a tube of wool jersey with heavy rayon thread, then shaping and hand-tacking. (Fig. 5-61)

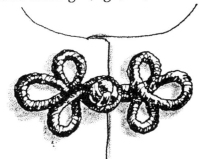

Fig. 5-61: *Make your own decorative frog closures with puffed serged braid.*

1. Create at least 1 yard of puffed braid following the previous instructions.

2. Cut a 10-1/2" strip and a 22" strip using the best sections of the braid. Apply seam sealant to each end and allow it to dry.

3. From the short strip, form four decorative loops, as shown. (Fig. 5-62) Hand-tack the braid together on the underside.

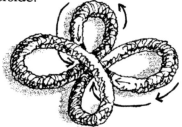

Fig. 5-62: *Form the looped side of the closure and hand-tack the ends.*

4. Using the longer strip, make a button with three decorative loops matching those in step 3. (Fig. 5-63) Hand-tack the braid together from the wrong side.

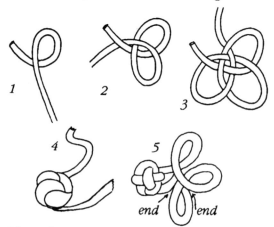

Fig. 5-63: *Make a ball button, then form the tail into three decorative loops.*

Project: Luxurious Lingerie Roll-up

Carry your lingerie in this elegant satin case while you travel. It's so pretty, you'll want to use it at home, too. (Fig. 5-64)

Fig. 5-64: *Protect delicate lingerie from snags or pulls in a serge-decorated case.*

Foot: None for braid; standard for serge-finishing
Stitch: 3-thread
Stitch length: Medium for braid; short for serge-finishing
Stitch width: Widest
Thread: Matching or contrasting color
  Needle: All-purpose or serger
  Upper looper: Heavy rayon, like Decor 6 or pearl rayon
  Lower looper: Woolly nylon for braid; matching heavy rayon for serge-finishing
Tension: Balanced, with lower looper slightly tightened for braid; balanced for serge-finishing
Needle: Size 11/75
Fabric: 1 yard heavy satin; 1"-wide strip of 60"-wide wool or acrylic jersey, cut on the crosswise grain

1. Create puffed braid from the jersey strip, following the previous instructions.

2. Cut two 10-1/2" strips of the braid. Apply seam sealant to each end and allow it to dry.

3. From one of the strips, form a decorative loop, as described under Frog Closures. From the other strip, form a button as described, but do not form the tails into loops; they will be shorter and used to attach the button. On both the loops and the button, hand-tack the braid together from the wrong side.

4. Cut two 12" by 36" satin rectangles, and place them wrong sides together.

5. With decorative thread in both loopers, serge around the entire rectangle, beginning at the center of the lower short edge. Begin and end the decorative serging using the hidden lapped serging technique, page 32.

6. Fold 8" toward the center on both ends, as shown. (Fig. 5-65) Top-stitch the pockets in place on both sides along the needlelines of the decorative serging.

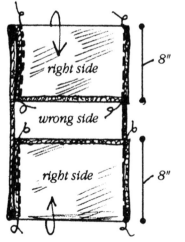

Fig. 5-65: Fold 8" pockets on both ends and top-stitch them in place.

7. Fold again at the edge of the top pocket, overlapping half of the lower pocket. Hand-tack the frog loops to the center of the upper flap and the ball button to the lower pocket. (Fig. 5-66)

Fig. 5-66: Hand-tack both sides of the frog closure to the bag.

Lesson 21.
Serged Picot Braid

Create a delicate but stable picot braid by serging on water-soluble stabilizer. Using a heavy decorative thread in the upper looper and monofilament nylon thread in the lower looper creates the appearance of a looped single strand. After zigzagging along the needleline and washing away the stabilizer, the braid may be glued to an accessory or craft project or top-stitched to a feminine blouse or dress.

Single-picot braid

1. Thread your serger with pearl cotton or crochet thread in the upper looper, monofilament nylon in the lower looper, and all-purpose or serger thread in the needle. Adjust for the longest, widest, balanced, 3-thread stitch. For maximum width, try removing the upper looper thread from the tension discs (see page 24).

2. Serge-finish a strip of water-soluble stabilizer. (For a long strand of braid, cut more than one stabilizer strip and lap the short ends during serging to reach the length desired.) To secure the serging, zigzag over the needleline with a narrow stitch and matching thread. (Fig. 5-67)

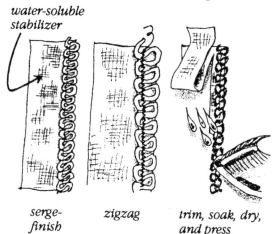

water-soluble stabilizer

serge-finish   zigzag   trim, soak, dry, and press

Fig. 5-67: *To make picot braid, serge-finish water-soluble stabilizer. Zigzag over the needleline, trim the excess stabilizer, and soak the braid before drying and pressing.*

3. Trim the stabilizer about 1/8" from the serging.

4. Soak the braid in cold or lukewarm water, then lay it flat on a paper towel to dry. Or blot the braid with a paper towel to remove most of the moisture and dry it in a microwave oven on a medium power setting for approximately two minutes. (For safety, set the timer for one-minute intervals or less and check after each period.) Make sure the braid is as flat as possible while drying. When dry, press the braid flat using a press cloth.

Double-picot braid

Two rows of single-picot stitches combine to form a wider, double-picot braid.

1. Complete steps 1 and 2 for single-picot braid.

2. Turn the strip in the opposite direction and serge a second row with the needleline right next to or on top of the first needleline. (You will be trimming off all the excess stabilizer as you serge this second row.) (Fig. 5-68)

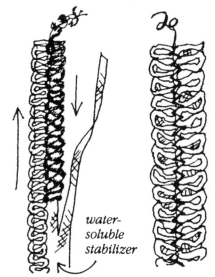

water-soluble stabilizer

Fig. 5-68: *Serge double-picot braid by overlapping the needlelines of two single-picot rows. Then zigzag over the needlelines before washing out the stabilizer.*

3. To stabilize the braid, zigzag the needlelines together with a narrow stitch and matching thread.

4. Finish by following step 4 for single picot braid.

Picot-braid variations

■ Use finer thread and a shorter stitch for a fluffier effect. Test the finer decorative thread in both loopers for a thicker braid.

■ Try various length, width, and tension settings, as well as different thread types and combinations.

■ For fusible picot braid, use fusible thread in the bobbin of the zigzag stitch. Using a press cloth, fuse the braid in place on the garment or project.

■ Save a step by zigzagging the braid to a washable project or garment fabric during step 3 of both the single- and double-picot braids. Then moisten or wash the entire piece to remove the excess stabilizer.

Stretch picot braid

Add stretch to your picot braid by serging it over transparent elastic as well as water-soluble stabilizer. This decorative, elasticized braid is perfect for hiding top-stitched hems and edges on swimsuits and exercisewear.

1. Complete step 1 for single picot braid.

2. Position 1/4"-wide transparent elastic over a 1"-wide strip of water-soluble stabilizer. Serge over both layers, just catching the needle in the edge of the elastic and stretching the elastic slightly as you serge. (Fig. 5-69)

3. After serging one side, turn the braid around and serge the other side with the needle next to the needleline of the previous stitching. Rinse out the stabilizer and allow the strip to dry.

4. Secure the braid to a stretch-fabric garment using a narrow zigzag stitch over the braid needlelines.

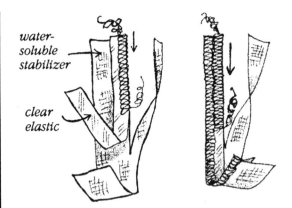

water-soluble stabilizer

clear elastic

Fig. 5-69: *Serge stretch picot braid over clear elastic and water-soluble stabilizer. Overlap needlelines on the second row.*

Project: Picot-braid Placemat

Double-picot braid adds a special, hand-crafted touch to a plain, inexpensive placemat. (Fig. 5-70)

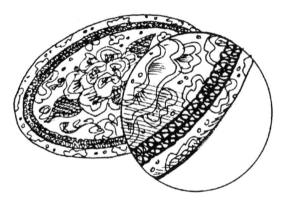

Fig. 5-70: *Top-stitch double-picot braid around the edge to dress up a placemat.*

Foot: Standard
Stitch: 3-thread
Stitch length: Longest
Stitch width: Widest
Thread: Contrasting color
   Needle: All-purpose or serger
   Upper looper: Pearl cotton or
     crochet thread
   Lower looper: Monofilament nylon
Tension: Balanced
Needle: Size 11/75
Notions: One purchased oval place-
   mat (or make one if you have time);
   6" by 27" piece of water-soluble
   stabilizer

N **Note:** One placemat will need approximately 1-1/2 yards of braid. Serge 7 yards for four placemats and select the best lengths for your project.

1. Thread and adjust your serger for picot braid following the previous instructions. Serge-finish one long edge of the stabilizer until you have enough yardage for your project.

2. Make double-picot braid by turning the strip in the opposite direction and serging a second row along the first needleline.

3. Zigzag over the needleline with a narrow stitch and matching thread.

4. Soak the braid to remove the stabilizer. Then dry and press the braid.

5. Top-stitch the picot braid onto the placemat, following a line of top-stitching or the inner edge of a binding strip. Begin and end in the center of the lower edge, tucking the ends under about 3/8".

Lesson 22. Serged Couching Braid

Couching braid (for embellishing fabric with curved or looped designs) can be created on your serger. In Lesson 20 (page 98), we featured puffed serged braid—one of our favorites for couched monograms and other designs.

Create a simpler, thread-chain couching braid by serging over a filler, such as strands of heavier thread or cord, using a rolled-edge stitch. Use heavier decorative thread in the upper looper and matching all-purpose or serger thread in the needle and lower looper. Place the filler under the back and over the front of the presser foot (or use a beading or ribbon foot), guiding it with the filler-cord techniques from Lesson 4 (page 48).

For a thinner couching braid, use a lighter-weight filler or fewer filler threads. If you use heavy thread in the upper looper, you may choose not to have a filler at all. Adjust your serger for a short, medium-width or narrower, balanced, 3-thread stitch. Tighten the lower looper slightly. The lower looper thread should not show, and any filler should be covered entirely by the upper looper thread.

Sew couching braid to your fabric by straight-stitching through it, zigzagging over it, or stitching beside it with a sewing machine blindhem stitch. Straight-stitching works best on thinner, flatter braid. You will often need to blindhem-stitch or zigzag over a thicker

Fig. 5-71: *Straight-stitch flatter couching braid. Zigzag or blindhem-stitch over thicker braid.*

braid. (Fig. 5-71) Use monofilament nylon or matching thread in the needle.

To apply couching directly with your serger, use a balanced or flatlock stitch. This application requires straighter design lines, but loops can be formed in the couching braid to add interest. The loops are later glued, hand-tacked, straight-stitched, or zigzagged down. (Fig. 5-72) You may also choose to thread a bead on the loop as you work, before securing the second side.

S **Special Tip:** For easier couching application, use a fusible thread in the lower looper when making the thread-chain couching braid. Loosen the lower looper tension enough for maximum thread coverage on the underside of the braid without having it visible on the top side. Fuse the braid to your fabric to complete the couching. For more durability after fusing, zigzag over the braid.

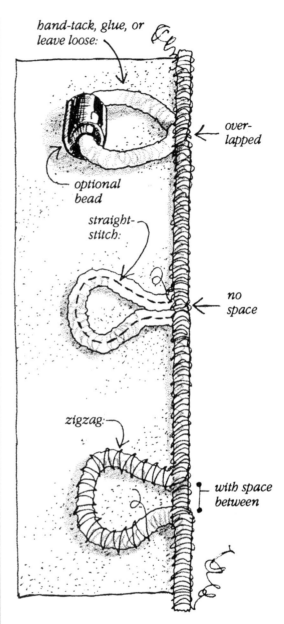

hand-tack, glue, or leave loose:

optional bead

over-lapped

straight-stitch:

no space

zigzag:

with space between

Fig. 5-72: *Serge-couch a straight edge, leaving loops. Variations add interest.*

Stretched couching braid

Another of our favorite couching braids is serged using a base of water-soluble stabilizer. It is flat and wider than puffed serged braid or thread-chain braid and, after moistening to remove the stabilizer, can be accurately preshaped into any design and dried before couching it to the fabric.

1. Adjust for the widest, satin-length, balanced, 3-thread stitch with pearl cotton (or other similar heavy thread) in both loopers and all-purpose or serger thread in the needle.

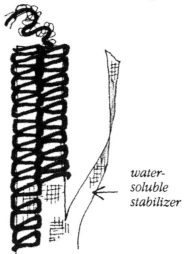

Note: Remember that the thread used for this braid must be washable because it will be moistened to remove the stabilizer.

2. Serge-finish a strip of water-soluble stabilizer, then turn the strip in the opposite direction and serge a second row with the needleline on top of or to the left of the first needleline. (You will be trimming off all the excess stabilizer as you serge this second row.) (Fig. 5-73)

water-
soluble
stabilizer

Fig. 5-73: Serge two rows of couching braid, overlapping the needlelines.

For a long strand of braid, cut more than one stabilizer strip and lap the short ends during serging to reach the length desired.

3. If you want to make a wider couching braid, serge again along one or both sides of the braid, with the needle inside the loops of one of the original rows.

4. Gently stretch the serged braid to set the stitches—it will be lengthened and narrowed. (On longer braid sections, start at the end and carefully slide the stitches along the needleline when stretching.) Then moisten the braid to remove the excess stabilizer and shape the braid into any design before drying. (Fig. 5-74) Because the dried braid holds its shape well, it's easy to create any letter or shape, including mirror-image designs for couching onto opposite sides of a garment.

Fig. 5-74: After stretching and moistening, shape the braid into a letter or design, then let dry.

5. Tuck under both unfinished, narrow ends of the braid, then top-stitch it (around all edges) to your garment or project.

Project: Monogrammed Shoe Tote

Use stretched couching braid to personalize a handy shoe tote. Your golfing or jogging friends will appreciate this thoughtful gift. (Fig. 5-75)

Fig. 5-75: *Two separate pockets on this monogrammed tote transport shoes neatly and in style.*

Foot: Standard
Stitch: 3-thread
Stitch length: Satin for braid; medium for serge-seaming and serge-finishing
Stitch width: Widest
Thread: Contrasting for braid; matching for serge-seaming and serge-finishing
Needle: All-purpose or serger

Upper looper: Heavy decorative (washable), such as pearl cotton, for braid; all-purpose or serger for serge-seaming and serge-finishing
Lower looper: Heavy decorative (washable), such as pearl cotton, for braid; all-purpose or serger for serge-seaming and serge-finishing
Tension: Balanced
Needle: Size 14/90
Fabric: 2 yards cotton canvas, cotton duck, or heavy nylon (45" width makes three totes)
Notions: 1/2 yard 1"-wide cotton or nylon webbing; one strip water-soluble stabilizer, the length of the serged couching braid; small piece of white freezer paper

I. Determine the letter or letters you'll be monogramming and draw them (or trace them from a pattern or stencil) onto white freezer paper to make a pattern. Measure the distance to be monogrammed.

2. Serge a double row of stretched couching braid over the water-soluble stabilizer following the previous instructions. Make enough to cover the monogram.

3. Starting from the front end of the braid, gently stretch it. Then moisten it, blot out the excess water, and shape it on top of the pattern.

4. Cut one 12" by 72" rectangle from the fabric.

5. Serge-finish both short ends of the rectangle. On each end, turn 1/2" to the wrong side and top-stitch.

6. After the braid is dry, place the monogram on the tote, positioning it on the right side, about 8" down from the top edge. Tuck the braid ends under and top-stitch around all edges.

7. With right sides together, fold 16" toward the center at each end. In the exact center of the rectangle, place the webbing against the sides on the right side, matching the cut edges. Serge-seam both long edges, catching the webbing in the serging. (Fig. 5-76)

8. Turn the pockets and handle right side out. Press the serge-finished edges toward the center on both sides of the tote. Edge-stitch to secure them and reinforce the handle. (Fig. 5-77)

Fig. 5-77: After turning the pockets and handle right side out, fold and straight-stitch the serge-finished edges on the right side.

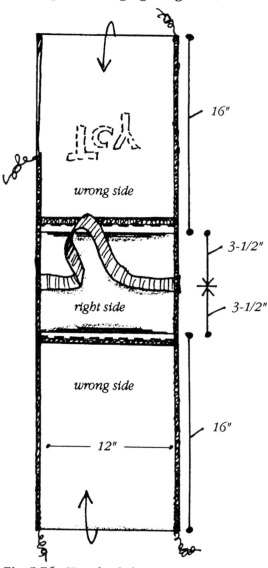

Fig. 5-76: Turn back the pockets and center the webbing handle before serging the sides.

6. Special Decorative Serging Techniques

In past lessons you've mastered seams, edges, bindings, braids, and other trims. Now it's time to explore some of the special decorative techniques that make serger sewing so much fun. You can embellish fabric with flatlocking, trims, beading, and couching. You can gather, shirr, and fringe. You can even make a delicate, tatting-like lace with serger stitches.

Although decoratively serging seams and edges can ornament your latest fashion garments in high style, many more options are available as well. By serging along folds, you can add embellishment anywhere on your fabric. Practically any decorative technique you see in ready-to-wear can be duplicated.

The lessons in this chapter will lead you through some of our favorite serger applications. You'll be delighted with the number of additional ornamental serging possibilities they open up for you.

Lesson 23. Gathering and Shirring

We use several different methods of serge-gathering to create ruffles, attach full skirts to waistbands or bodices, and to ornament other serger projects. Although generally fast and easy, serge-gathering works best on projects that do not require the wider seam allowances used for couture tailoring or delicate fabrics.

The width of the serge-gathered seam allowance is limited by the width of the serged stitch. The weight or thickness of your fabric and the project itself help determine what method to use. With serge-gathering, a single layer of fabric will gather more than multiple layers.

Tension gathering

For easy gathering of lightweight fabric, tighten the needle tension almost all the way. Use a long stitch, your widest width, and a balanced, 3-thread stitch. If you are using two needles, tighten both needle tensions. Vary the amount of gathers by changing the stitch length. A longer stitch will gather the fabric more.

For speedier tension gathering, instead of tightening the tension controls, press the needle thread(s) against the face of your serger, as shown. (Fig. 6-1) Test

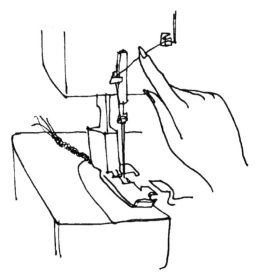

Fig. 6-1: *To quickly gather lightweight fabric, apply tension to the needle thread(s).*

this on your model to determine where to press for the best effect. This instant finger tensioning returns to normal just by releasing the threads.

Differential-feed gathering

If your serger has differential feed, you can use it to easily gather lightweight fabrics. Use a wide, medium-length, balanced stitch. Adjust the differential feed to 2.0 for serge-gathering. To vary the amount of gathers, change the differential-feed setting or the length of the stitch.

To softly gather or ease only one layer when you are serging two layers, lengthen the stitch. With the differential feed on 2.0, hold the top layer taut, away from the under layer. On light- to medium-weight fabrics, the under layer will gather as you serge it to the top layer. Softer fabrics will gather more than stiff fabrics. Shorten your stitch length to reduce the amount of gathering.

Filler-cord gathering

To serge-gather medium- to heavy-weight fabrics, serge over a strand of filler cord such as buttonhole twist, crochet thread, or pearl cotton. (Fig. 6-2) Use a

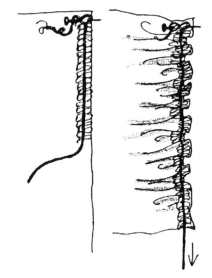

Fig. 6-2: *For medium- to heavy-weight fabric, serge over filler cord and pull to gather.*

wide, medium-length (or shorter), balanced, 3- or 3/4-thread stitch. Place the filler under the back and over the front of the presser foot (or use a beading or ribbon foot), guiding it with the techniques from Lesson 4 (page 48). Serge over the filler, being careful not to cut it. Secure one end of the filler and pull the other end to gather the edge.

If your serger has a 3/4-thread stitch, you can use both needles as you serge. Guide the filler between the needles. (Fig. 6-3) The needle threads hold the filler in position for more controlled gathering.

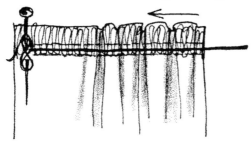

Fig. 6-3: *For more controlled gathering, place the filler thread between the two needles of a 3/4-thread stitch.*

Thread-chain gathering

This technique uses thread chain as a gathering filler cord. Serge off a thread chain that is slightly longer than the edge to be gathered. Raise the presser foot and bring the chain under the back and over the front of the foot (or use a beading or ribbon foot). Insert the fabric under the foot and serge over the chain, using a 3-thread stitch, as if you were using filler thread. Then pull the chain to gather. Or hold the chain taut to gather as you serge.

Serge-shirring

Parallel rows of serge-shirring can create a stretchy waistband or cuffs on your latest fashion garments. We prefer to shirr the fabric first, before cutting it out. In addition to gathering the fabric length-wise, the serge-shirred stitching takes up extra fabric width—about twice the width

of the serged stitch for each row of shirring.

For easiest serge-shirring, begin with a long strip of elastic thread, cording, or narrow clear elastic. (For more durability when shirring with elastic thread, serge over two or more strands.) Mark the desired length of your finished shirring on the elastic using a marking pen. Leave some extra elastic at the beginning end. After serge-shirring over the elastic and fabric (see the instructions following), secure the beginning end of the elastic by pinning or sewing it, and gather from the opposite end. (Fig. 6-4)

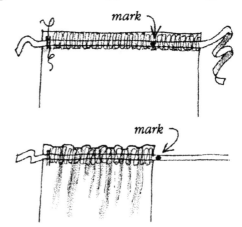

Fig. 6-4: *Shirr accurately by marking the desired length on the elastic. Serge over the elastic, secure one end, and gather to the mark.*

Because you've serged over the elastic, not into it, it will pull easily. When the mark is exposed, secure and trim that end of the elastic and adjust the shirring evenly.

To serge-shirr using **elastic thread** or **cording**, adjust your serger for a medium-width, medium-length, balanced, 3-thread stitch. To serge-shirr with 1/8" **clear elastic,** use a wide stitch instead. Place the elastic under the back and over the front of the presser foot (or use a beading or ribbon foot) as for the filler-cord gathering on page 110.

To begin, serge several stitches over the elastic until you reach the first mark. Fold the fabric right sides together and place it under the presser foot. Serge over the folded edge, being careful not to cut the fabric or elastic. Secure one end of the elastic by pinning or sewing it, then pull up the elastic to complete the shirring.

For more controlled shirring, serge over elastic thread using a 3/4-thread stitch. Feed the elastic thread between the two needles, as for the 3/4-thread filler cord application (see page 111). The shirring will be a little bulkier and will require more fabric because of the wider stitch, but it will remain more evenly distributed during wearing.

An optional shirring method is to serge through a strip of 1/4"- or 3/8"-wide clear elastic, stretching the elastic as you serge. Adjust your serger for a medium stitch width and long stitch length. Thread the elastic under the back and over the front of the foot or use a ribbon or elastic foot for easier guiding. Evenly section and mark the elastic and the fabric, leaving a section for starting in front of the first mark on the elastic. Serge a few stitches on the elastic, then insert the folded fabric matching the first marks. Serge, stretching the elastic to match the section marks, as shown. (Fig. 6-5)

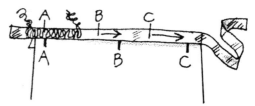

Fig. 6-5: *Shirr while serging by stretching clear elastic to meet presectioned markings.*

S **Special Tip:** When using an elastic foot, thread the elastic through the foot and out and under the back before attaching the foot to the machine. Before shirring your project, test the foot adjustment on a project scrap until you reach the desired amount of stretch.

Double chainstitch shirring

Serge-shirring may also be done using the 2-thread double chainstitch, if that option is available on your model. Thread elastic cording in the looper and adjust for a long stitch. Loosen both the needle and looper tensions slightly. Serge rows of shirring, using the presser foot to guide the width of the rows. For ease in handling multiple rows of serge-shirring, serge them over a strip of adding-machine tape or freezer paper. Tear away the paper after serging.

Project:
Fluffy Nylon Sponges

These quick and easy sponges are one of the most useful items you can add to your household or give as a gift. Use them for everything from dishwashing and cleaning the tub to buffing your face or decorating the Christmas tree. (Fig. 6-6)

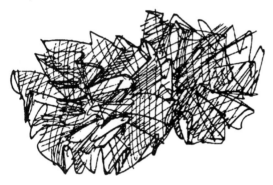

Fig. 6-6: Quick-drying nylon-netting sponges have a multitude of uses.

Foot: Standard
Stitch: 3-thread
Stitch length: Medium
Stitch width: Medium
Thread: Matching
    Needle: All-purpose or serger
    Upper looper: All-purpose or
      serger
    Lower looper: All-purpose or
      serger
Tension: Balanced
Needle: Size 11/75
Fabric: Two 4"-wide crosswise strips
    of nylon net (72"-wide)
Notions: Pearl cotton

1. Allowing a 2" tail, thread two strands of pearl cotton under the back and over the front of the presser foot (see filler-cord gathering, page 110). Serge several stitches over the pearl cotton with a medium-width, balanced stitch.

2. Fold one net strip in half lengthwise. Insert the netting under the presser foot and serge over it along the folded edge.

When you reach the end of one strip, fold the other strip in half and butt it to the end of the first strip. (Fig. 6-7) Continue serging over the fold until the end of the second strip.

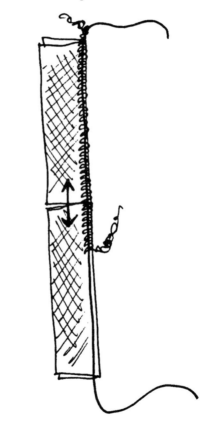

Fig. 6-7: Butt the two folded netting strips end-to-end and continuously serge-gather the folded edge.

3. Secure one end of the pearl cotton. Pull the opposite end to tightly gather the netting.

4. Tie the pearl cotton ends into a secure knot and trim away the excess.

Optional: To add a pretty hanger to the sponge, use narrow ribbon in place of the pearl cotton. After drawing up the net and tying a secure knot, tie the ribbon ends into a loop with a bow at the top. (Fig. 6-8)

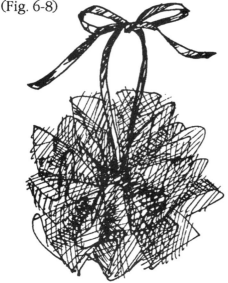

Fig. 6-8: Serge-gather over a narrow ribbon, then knot a loop and a bow for a decorative hanger.

Lesson 24. Serger Lace

One of our favorite details for finishing dainty tucks on garment fronts and collars, serger lace also has interesting applications on numerous craft and accessory projects.

This lace is made by merely overlapping rows of balanced, 3-thread serging. The appearance of serger lace can be varied by the thread used in the loopers and the number of rows of serging (more rows create a wider lace). Using buttonhole twist will give the look of a hand-crocheted edge. Lightweight thread creates a more delicate effect.

1. Adjust your serger for the longest, widest, 3-thread stitch. You may want to loosen the needle tension slightly.

2. Serge one row of stitching to the fabric, allowing all but the needleline to hang off the edge. Leave at least a 4" thread chain at each end.

3. Overlap a second row of serging with the needle inside the overlocking loops of the first row of stitching. (Fig. 6-9) For accuracy, mark the needleline

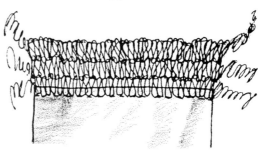

Fig. 6-9: Overlap rows of 3-thread serging to form lace.

on the presser foot (if it isn't already), using a fine-tipped permanent marking pen. Align the loops with the mark when adding additional rows.

4. To make wider lace, continue overlapping rows of serging to the width desired. It may take a little practice to position the needle just inside the loops. If the needle misses stitching inside the loops, you will have a hole in the lace. In this case, simply find the shortest thread (the needle thread) and pull it. The loops will fall away from the previous stitching, and you can serge the row again.

5. To widen the lace after serging, gently pull it crosswise, away from the fabric. If you want to ruffle the lace, gently stretch it parallel to the edge. (Fig. 6-10)

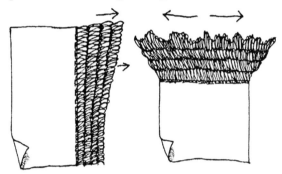

Fig. 6-10: Gently pull the lace crosswise to widen it. Stretch it parallel to the edge to ruffle it.

Stabilized lace

Make a perfect serged-lace edge with water-soluble stabilizer as a base.

1. Serge-finish the fabric edge.

2. Cut a piece of stabilizer four times the finished width by the finished length of the lace you'll be making.

3. Adjust your serger for the longest, widest, balanced, 3-thread stitch.

4. Place the stabilizer on the wrong side of the finished fabric, allowing it to extend 1/4" beyond the edge. Serge with the needleline just inside the loops of the previous stitching. (Fig. 6-11)

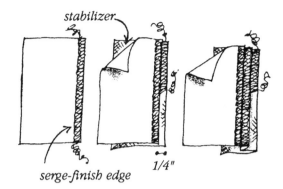

Fig. 6-11: Add stabilized lace to a fabric edge. Serge-finish the edge. Place water-soluble stabilizer underneath, extending 1/4" beyond the edge. Serge, catching the needleline inside the previous stitching. Fold the stabilizer and repeat for the desired width. Spray or soak to remove the stabilizer.

5. Fold the stabilizer to the right of the serging. Then refold the stabilizer back, leaving a stitch width of stabilizer to the right of the stitching, as shown.

6. Serge over the fold with the needleline just inside the loops of the previous stitching. Repeat for each additional row until the lace is the desired width.

7. Carefully spray the lace or soak it in water to remove the stabilizer. Allow the lace to air dry or dry it in the microwave on medium power, setting the timer for one-minute intervals and checking after each minute. When dry, the lace will have a starched feel. To soften, carefully manipulate the lace with your fingers.

Make a strip of stable lace trim following the same procedure. Begin with steps 2 and 3 for serger lace. Serge-finish one long edge of the stabilizer, then follow steps 5 through 7 to complete the trim. (Fig. 6-12)

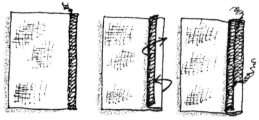

Fig. 6-12: *Make stable lace trim by serging one edge of the stabilizer, folding it to the right and refolding to leave a stitch-width to the right. Serge the new fold with the needle just inside the previous stitch. Repeat for the width desired.*

Serger lace tucks

For accuracy, serge lace tucks onto the fabric before cutting out the project. Begin by folding the fabric on the first tuck line. Serge-finish the edge with the needle about 1/8" inside the fold. Allow the loops to hang off the edge of the fabric. (Use a blindhem foot, if available, to ensure even stitching.) Continue folding and serging the tucks, using the presser foot to guide your stitching evenly. (Fig. 6-13) For wider

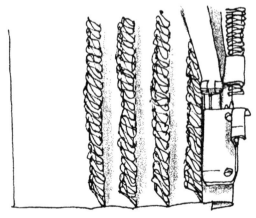

Fig. 6-13: *Serge even lace tucks by guiding the presser-foot edge along the previous row.*

lace tucks, serge another row of stitching inside the first row of loops. Delicate care may be required for this wider lace.

Lacy fishline ruffles

To add a lace finish on the edge of fishline ruffles, apply the fishline according to the instructions in Lesson 6 (page 56). Serge the first row of lace with the needle just inside the rolled edge. Serge additional rows for wider lace.

Lace-trimmed wires

Serger lace also can be used to trim fine, flexible wires for craft projects. Cover the wire with a narrow, rolled-edge stitch. For the easiest application, use a beading foot (see Lesson 7, page 56). Or guide the wire under the presser foot between the needle and the knife, **serging slowly.**

Adjust for a wide, long, balanced, 3-thread stitch. Serge over the covered wire, keeping it between the needle and the knife, with the stitch loops hanging off the edge.

Serge additional rows to make wider lace. Shape the lace-trimmed wire as desired and twist the ends together.

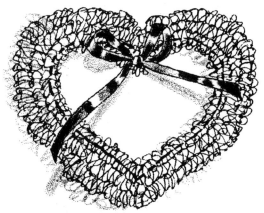

Fig. 6-14: Serge lace over covered wire and shape as desired.

(Fig. 6-14) Secure all the thread ends with seam sealant.

Project: Lace-edged Pocket Hanky

Overlap rows of serger lace on the edge of a circular hanky. When picked up in the center, the decorative lace edge drapes into attractive folds. (Fig. 6-15)

Fig. 6-15: Rows of serged buttonhole-twist lace edge a feminine pocket hanky.

Foot: Standard
Stitch: 3-thread
Stitch length: Long
Stitch width: Medium to wide
Thread: Matching or contrasting color
    Needle: All-purpose or serger
    Upper looper: Buttonhole twist
    Lower looper: Buttonhole twist
Tension: Balanced with all tensions loosened
Needle: Size 11/75
Fabric: 1/3 yard 45"-wide batiste

1. Cut one 12" circle of the batiste, using a plate as a guide.

2. Apply serger lace to the circular edge, following the previous instructions. After serge-finishing the fabric edge, overlap the stitches for about 1/2", then angle upward and begin a second row. Apply a dab of seam sealant to the overlapped stitches before continuing.

3. Slowly complete a second and third row of lace, serging continuously. (Fig. 6-16)

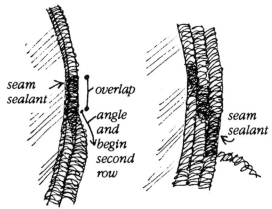

seam sealant → overlap

angle and begin second row

seam sealant

Fig. 6-16: Overlap each row of serger lace for about 1/2", then angle into the next row. After three rows, overlap into the previous stitching. Use seam sealant on the beginning and ending overlaps.

4. Blend the end of the third row into the previous stitches. Dab the joint with seam sealant, and trim the thread ends when dry.

Lesson 25. Decorative Flatlocking

In Lesson 3, we discussed basic flatlocking as it relates to flatlocked seams. Flatlocking also can be applied on folds, so it can be used as decorative detailing anywhere on a garment or project. Among its varied applications, flatlocking can be stitched at angles across the front of an embellished sweatshirt or added as a delicate accent on dressier cuffs and collars.

For the following techniques, unless otherwise specified, it is assumed that your serger is adjusted to basic flatlocking tensions and that you will use either 2- or 3-thread flatlocking. (See page 43 for details.) Loosen the needle tension enough to allow the serging to pull flat after being stitched. For 3-thread flatlocking, tighten the lower looper until it forms a straight line.

N **Note:** The following decorative flatlocking techniques give instructions for 3-thread flatlocking because it is the most widely available option. If you'll be using 2-thread flatlocking instead, put the thread specified for the upper looper in the lower looper and use the needle thread indicated.

For most flatlocking, it is not necessary to disengage the knife. Simply move the fabric fold to the left of the knife about half of the stitch width. This also allows the stitches to hang off the edge for the flattest flatlocking. Use a blindhem foot, if available, to stitch accurately. Place the fold of the fabric against the foot's guide, and adjust the guide so that the fold is positioned in the center of the stitching.

In addition to basic flatlocking, other novelty flatlocking effects can be achieved by changing tensions, stitch widths, and thread types.

Floating Flatlocking

To make a flatlock stitch appear to float on top of the fabric, use monofilament nylon thread in the needle and lower looper. Put a heavy decorative thread in the upper looper. For maximum emphasis, adjust for the widest and longest possible stitch. (Fig. 6-17)

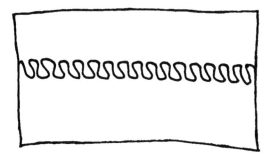

Fig. 6-17: Float the upper looper thread on top of the fabric by flatlocking with monofilament nylon in the needle and lower looper.

Corded flatlocking

Flatlocking does not always require a wide stitch width. Narrow, satin-stitch flatlocking gives the appearance of cording or piping. For a more corded effect, use a narrow stitch and tighten the needle tension slightly to raise the

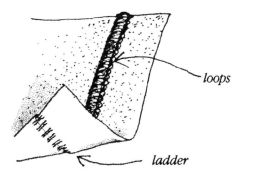

Fig. 6-18: *For corded flatlocking, tighten the needle tension.*

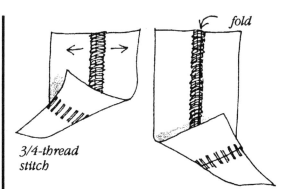

3/4-thread
stitch

Fig. 6-19: *Loosen both needle tensions for safety-stitch flatlocking. With slightly tighter tension, a fold forms underneath the loops.*

stitch. (Fig. 6-18) Shorten the stitch length for maximum thread coverage. A narrow ladder stitch will show from the underside. For the narrowest corded flatlocking, use the rolled-edge stitch finger.

Safety-stitch flatlocking

Flatlock with a wide, 3/4-thread stitch for safety-stitched flatlocking. Use a short- to medium-length, wide stitch and loosen both needle tensions. (Fig. 6-19) On the underside, the ladder stitch will look similar to a 2- or 3-thread flatlock. The loops on the top side will have an extra right needle-thread line showing. Adjust to the widest setting, and make sure both needles are serging on the fabric.

If you are unable to loosen your needle tensions enough, safety-stitch flatlocking may not pull completely flat. An option for this stitch is to create a raised fold underneath the flatlocked loops using a slightly tighter needle tension. (Fig. 6-19)

Balanced flatlocking

Basic 3-thread flatlocking can be adjusted so the looper tensions are balanced, with the upper and lower looper stitches overlocking in the center of the stitch. (Fig. 6-20)

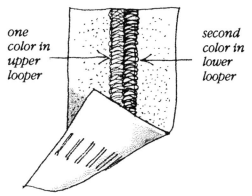

one
color in
upper
looper

second
color in
lower
looper

Fig. 6-20: *Flatlocking with balanced looper tensions creates a two-toned stitch.*

Adjust for 3-thread flatlocking, then tighten the upper looper tension and loosen the lower looper tension. The needle tension remains loose so the stitch will lie flat. Use contrasting thread colors in the loopers for a multi-colored stitch.

Mock hemstitching

For mock hemstitching, simply straight-stitch through the center of a wide, flatlocked stitch. For the ladder side out, flatlock with right sides together. Pull the fabric flat. Top-stitch from the wrong side with monofilament nylon thread in the bobbin and thread that matches the fabric in the needle. (Fig. 6-21) The ladder stitches will

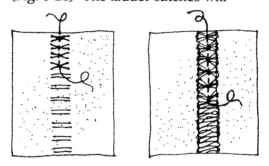

ladder on right side   *loops on right side*

Fig. 6-21: *Straight-stitch either the looped or ladder side of the flatlocking to create mock hemstitching.*

automatically bunch together. With this stitch, the serger needle thread is the ladder thread that shows, so the decorative thread you use must be able to be threaded through the needle. Experiment with the stitch length for different effects.

Mock hemstitching also can be flatlocked with the looped side out. (Fig. 6-21) Use the decorative thread in the looper. Flatlock and then top-stitch from the ladder side with monofilament nylon thread in the bobbin and thread that matches the fabric in the needle.

Serge-fagoting

Fagoting is a decorative flatlock stitch used for fabric embellishment or seams when the area, such as the front of a blouse, will not be subjected to much stress. Most often used in heirloom serging on fine fabrics, fagoting is sewn with the ladder side out. Use decorative thread in the needle. For inconspicuous loops (they may be seen from the top side after the edges are pulled apart), use monofilament nylon thread in the upper looper.

If you apply serge-fagoting to your garment fabric before cutting it out, establish a fagoting seamline and cut along it. Serge-finish the seam allowances and press them to the wrong side. Adjust for a long, wide flatlock stitch. With right sides together and the folds aligned, flatlock with the needle barely catching the edge of the fabric. Pull the stitching flat and press carefully. (Fig. 6-22)

wrong side   *right side*

Fig. 6-22: *For serge-fagoting, press back the seam allowances. Flatlock, barely catching the folds. Then pull the stitches flat.*

For further embellishment, thread narrow ribbon through the ladder stitches. Securely top-stitch the seam allowances on both sides of the fagoting, using a decorative stitch on your sewing machine or a 2-thread double chainstitch. Then center your pattern over the yardage and cut it out.

Project: The Flatlocked Cat

Practice your flatlocking skills on this charming sampler. The helpful kitty stands as a reminder of stitch options available for your future projects. (Fig. 6-23)

Fig. 6-23: *This flatlocking-sampler cat can be used as a precious gift or keep it for your own sewing area.*

Foot: Blindhem or standard
Stitch: 3-thread
Stitch length: Short unless otherwise indicated
Stitch width: Widest unless otherwise indicated
Thread: Contrasting for flatlocking unless otherwise indicated; matching for serge-seaming
   Needle(s): All-purpose or serger unless otherwise indicated

   Upper looper: As indicated in instructions
   Lower looper: All-purpose or serger unless otherwise indicated
Tension: Basic flatlock unless otherwise indicated
Needle(s): Size 11/75
Fabric: 1/3 yard robe velour
Notions: 1 yard 3/16"-wide contrasting satin ribbon; polyester fiberfill for stuffing

1. Fold the center of the fabric on the bias with wrong sides together. Flatlock the fold with monofilament nylon thread in both loopers. You may need to loosen both tensions slightly. Thread the narrow ribbon under the monofilament loops.

 Note: In Lesson 27, you will learn how to flatlock over ribbon. You may want to substitute that technique for step 1, to avoid having to thread the ribbon under the loops after they are serged.

2. On both sides of the threaded flatlocking, serge a row of mock hemstitching a presser foot's width away. Serge with right sides together, buttonhole twist in the needle, and all-purpose or serger thread in the loopers. Topstitch through the center of the stitching from the wrong side, using monofilament nylon in the bobbin.

3. Continue placing rows of various stitch types a presser foot's width on either side of the previous rows. Next to the mock hemstitching, add a row of basic flatlocking. Use pearl rayon or another heavy decorative thread in the upper looper.

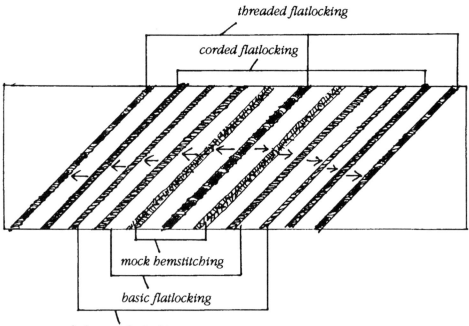

threaded flatlocking

corded flatlocking

mock hemstitching

basic flatlocking

balanced flatlocking

Fig. 6-24: *Starting from the center, flatlock bias rows of novelty stitches.*

4. Serge a row of balanced flatlocking on either side of the basic flatlocking, using contrasting colors of buttonhole twist in the loopers.

5. On either side of the balanced flatlocking, serge a row of narrow corded flatlocking. Use woolly nylon in the upper looper. (Fig. 6-24)

6. Serge another row of threaded flatlocking (see step 1) on either side of the corded flatlocking.

7. Make a cat pattern using the grid shown. (Fig. 6-25)

8. Cut the cat front from the flatlocked fabric. Cut the cat back, two tails, and one gusset from unembellished fabric.

9. Serge-seam the tail, right sides together. Use a medium-length, medium-width, balanced, 3-thread stitch and all-purpose thread. Leave an opening on the end to stuff the fiberfill.

10. Turn the tail right side out and stuff lightly. Pin the tail at the placement mark on the right side of the cat front piece.

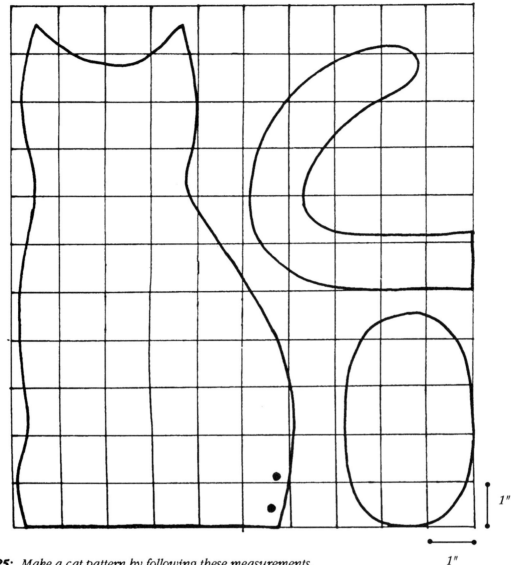

Fig. 6-25: *Make a cat pattern by following these measurements.*

1"

1"

11. With right sides together, serge-seam the sides and head of the cat, catching the open end of the tail in the stitching. Use the same serger settings as for step 9.

12. With right sides together, serge-seam the gusset to the lower cat edge, leaving a 2" opening along one straight side for turning and stuffing.

13. Turn the cat right side out and stuff. Hand-tack the opening closed and the end of the tail into a curled position on the front of the cat.

Lesson 26. Fringing

We see fringing on everything from scarves and garment edges to table-cloths and napkins. Using either flatlocking or balanced stitching, you can add a stable, decorative accent to the edge of any fringe. For fastest fringing, choose a fabric that ravels easily.

Flatlocked fringe

Choose balanced flatlocking or one of the other flatlocking options in Lesson 25.

1. Select the width of fringe desired and pull a thread or press to mark the lines—at least 1" from the edge.

2. Fold your fabric wrong sides together and flatlock over the fringe line with a short- to medium-length, medium-width stitch. Use a matching or contrasting thread color in both the upper looper and the needle.

3. Start at a corner where the marked lines intersect. Flatlock to the next intersection and (before turning) pull the previous stitching flat. (Fig. 6-26)

Fold the next side, turn the fabric a quarter turn, and repeat for the remaining sides.

4. Secure the ends by weaving the thread chains under the stitching.

5. For easiest fringing, clip from the cut edge to (but not through) the stitching every 2". Fringe to the stitching line by pulling out the horizontal threads.

Tucked fringe

For this edging option, serge a tuck and then top-stitch it down to the fabric, next to the area to be fringed.

1. Put decorative thread in the upper looper and adjust for a short, medium-width or wider, balanced, 3-thread stitch.

2. Pull a thread or press 1-1/4" away from the edges to mark the fringing lines.

3. Fold under 1-1/4" to the wrong side and, with the wrong side up, serge-finish along the fold to form a tuck. At the corner, serge to the intersection of the marked lines. Raise the presser foot, clear the stitches from the stitch

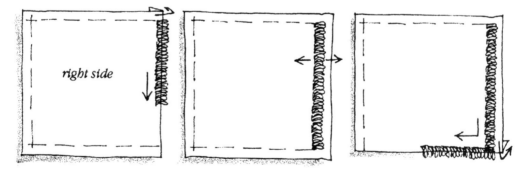

Fig. 6-26: *For flatlocked fringe, serge on the fold between the intersecting lines. Pull the stitching flat, turn the square corner, and repeat for the adjoining side.*

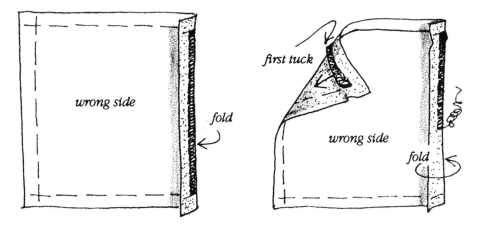

Fig. 6-27: *For tucked fringe, use a balanced stitch. Serge between the intersecting marks and fold the tuck toward the center. Repeat for the adjoining sides.*

finger, pull the fabric back behind the needle, and serge off. (Fig. 6-27)

4. Fold the serge-finished tuck away from the cut edge. Fold the adjoining edge along the marked line, in the same manner as for step 3. Clear the stitches from the stitch finger again and position the needle directly over the outside edge of the previous stitching. Begin by serging over the previous tuck, then continue serging the edge as in step 3.

5. Repeat steps 3 and 4 for the remaining edges to be fringed.

6. Press the finished tucks away from the edges. Hide the thread chains under the tucks and top-stitch to secure.

7. Clip the cut edges below the tucks every 2" and fringe by pulling out the horizontal threads.

Project: Fringed Cocktail Napkins

Tie up a stack of flatlock-fringed napkins for a much-appreciated hostess gift. (Fig. 6-28)

Fig. 6-28: *Practice flatlock fringing on a set of cocktail napkins. Do the serging quickly, then fringe while waiting for an appointment or watching TV.*

Foot: Standard
Stitch: 3-thread
Stitch length: Medium
Stitch width: Medium
Thread: Matching color
    Needle: Buttonhole twist
    Upper looper: Buttonhole twist
    Lower looper: All-purpose or
        serger
Tension: Balanced
Needle: Size 11/75
Fabric: 1/2 yard 45"-wide loosely
    woven cotton or cotton/polyester
Notions: 1-1/4 yard satin ribbon (for
    a tie)

1. Cut ten 8" napkin squares. Press-mark the fringe lines on all the squares 1" from each edge.

2. Flatlock over the fringe lines, following the previous instructions for flatlocked fringe.

3. Secure the thread ends and fringe to the stitching lines. Fold and stack the napkins and tie with the ribbon

Lesson 27.
Serging over Trim

If a decorative thread, yarn, or ribbon is too bulky (or not flexible enough) to thread through your loopers, you have the option of serging over it. To completely cover the trim width with serging, it must be narrow enough to fit between the needle and the knife. The upper looper also must be able to clear the trim without catching so the stitches can form evenly.

To serge over decorative trim, adjust for a stitch width wide enough to cover the trim. The length of the stitch will depend on how much of the trim you

want to expose. Start with a medium stitch length for testing. Use a balanced, 3-thread stitch or a 2- or 3-thread flatlock. Use monofilament nylon or matching all-purpose or serger thread in the upper looper to emphasize the trim.

Place the trim under the back and over the front of the presser foot (or use a beading or ribbon foot), guiding it with the filler-cord techniques from Lesson 4 (page 48). Remember to allow several inches of trim to extend behind the foot for easy starting.

For the easiest feeding, begin serging over the trim for several stitches with no fabric underneath. Then insert the fabric under the trim and serge **slowly.** Be careful not to stitch through the trim or cut it with the knives. Especially if it's bulky, you may need to hold the trim taut to guide it out from under the back of the presser foot.

Flatlocking over ribbon

Try flatlocking over a ribbon to cover a seam. The ribbon should be narrow enough to be serged over without cutting or stitching through it. A 7.5mm stitch width is just wide enough to cover a 1/4"-wide ribbon. For narrower stitch widths, use 3/16"- or 1/8"-wide ribbon. A 1/16"-wide ribbon is also available if you choose to use an even narrower stitch.

1. Serge-seam the fabric with right sides together.

2. Apply the ribbon following the instructions for serging over trim. A ribbon foot (see page 48) is specially designed to position ribbon for the easiest application.

3. Fold the fabric on the seamline, wrong sides together. Raise the presser foot and put the fabric halfway under the ribbon. Flatlock through all layers, with the stitches just covering the ribbon edges. (Fig. 6-29)

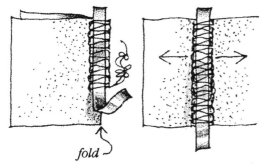

Fig. 6-29: *Center ribbon along the fabric fold before flatlocking. The stitches will hang off the edge. Pull flat.*

4. Pull the stitching flat and the ribbon will cover the seamline.

Flatlocking over lace and ribbon

Another decorative technique is to center a layer of double-edged lace over the seamline on the right side of the fabric. Then fold the lace and the fabric along the seamline and flatlock the ribbon on top (through all layers) using the previous method for flatlocking over trim and ribbon. (Fig. 6-30)

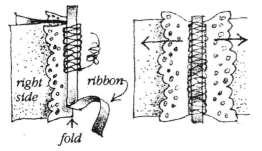

Fig. 6-30: *Flatlock to attach a layer of ribbon and lace to fabric.*

Flatlocking over yarn

Flatlocking over yarn with monofilament nylon thread appears to leave the yarn floating on the fabric surface.

1. Fold the fabric right sides together with the yarn inside the fold. (Fig. 6-31)

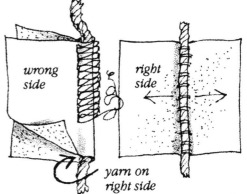

Fig. 6-31: *Flatlock over decorative yarn from the wrong side. Only the ladder stitch shows on the right side.*

2. Thread monofilament nylon in the needle and matching all-purpose or serger thread in the looper(s).

3. Serge the fold with a wide, long flatlock stitch.

4. Pull the fold flat. From the right side, the yarn floats on the surface, held invisibly by the monofilament.

Project:
Plush Velvet Muffler

Flatlock rows of ribbon to embellish the ends of this pretty muffler. Use it to dress up your everyday coat as well as for special occasions. (Fig. 6-32)

Fig. 6-32: Stay warm elegantly with a ribbon-trimmed, velvet muffler.

Foot: Ribbon or standard for ribbon application; standard for serge-seaming
Stitch: 3-thread
Stitch length: Long for flatlocking; medium for serge-seaming
Stitch width: Widest
Thread: Matching color
   Needle(s): All-purpose or serger
   Upper looper: Monofilament nylon for flatlocking; all-purpose or serger for serge-seaming
   Lower looper: All-purpose or serger

Tension: Flatlocking for ribbon application; balanced for serge-seaming
Needle(s): Size 11/75
Fabric: 2/3 yard 36"-wide velvet; 2/3 yard 45"-wide matching satin
Notions: 2 yards 3/16"-wide satin ribbon (1/8"-wide for narrower stitch widths); 1 yard 3/16"-wide velvet ribbon

1. Trim the satin to a 36" width. Cut both the velvet and the satin in half crosswise into two 12" by 36" strips.

2. On both the velvet and the satin, serge-seam two short ends with right sides together to make one long strip of each.

3. On the velvet strip, flatlock a satin ribbon 2" from the short ends. Flatlock velvet ribbon 1-1/2" inside the first ribbons and another row of satin ribbon 1" past both of those, as shown. (Fig. 6-33)

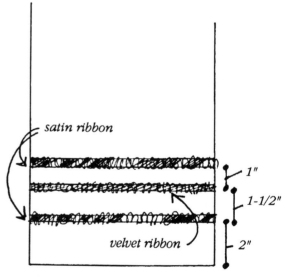

Fig. 6-33: Embellish the muffler by flatlocking over ribbon at both ends.

4. With the velvet and satin right sides together, serge-seam, leaving a 3" opening on one long edge for turning.

5. Turn the muffler right side out and hand-tack the opening closed.

Lesson 28.
Sequin, Bead, and Pearl Application

Strands of colorful beads, elegant pearls, and shiny sequins can be serged to edges or anywhere else on your garment or project. Use them for bridalwear, holiday glitz, or just for fun.

Applying beads and pearls

Beaded trims (available at craft and fabric stores or through mail order) can be applied with a flatlock, rolled edge, or even a balanced stitch. The beads must be small enough to fit between the needle and knife and for the upper looper to pass over them. Purchase enough yardage (at least three extra yards) for thorough testing before application.

Beads or sequins may be applied by removing the presser foot and guiding them manually between the needle and the knife. A beading foot simplifies the application for beads or sequins less than 1/4" wide.

1. If your machine has two needles, use the left needle for larger beads and the right needle for smaller beads.

2. Adjust for a stitch slightly longer and wider than the beads you are applying.

3. Use monofilament nylon thread (or matching all-purpose or serger thread)

in the upper looper and matching all-purpose or serger thread in the needle and lower looper.

N **Note:** Both a 2-thread flatlock and a 2-thread rolled edge work well for the application of bead trim, because less thread coverage provides a neat finish. For a 2-thread stitch, use the monofilament thread in the lower looper.

4. If you are attaching the beads to a fold, adjust for a flatlock stitch (see page 43). If you are attaching the beads to an edge, adjust for a rolled edge.

5. Attach a beading foot, if available, and place the bead strand along the right side of the foot so that it rests in the front guide and feeds under the back one. (Fig. 6-34) If you are serging

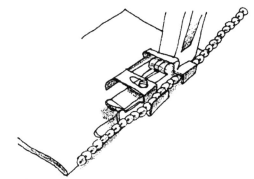

Fig. 6-34: Easily serge over beaded trim using a pearl/sequin or beading foot.

without a foot, position the beads between the needle and the knife. Allow 2" to 3" to extend beyond the back of the foot or past the needle.

6. Serge slowly over several inches of beading before inserting the fabric. Then guide the fabric fold or edge (bead stitching line) under the front of the foot (or under the beads if you're serging without a foot). When flatlocking over the beads, test to determine how far from the knife you'll guide the fabric before beginning your project. If you're guiding beads manually without the foot, remember to allow the beads and stitches to hang off the edge when using a flatlock stitch.

7. To serge off, cut the bead strand and carefully serge over the end. If necessary, use seam sealant to secure the beads before cutting.

Optional: For a heavier, beaded-crochet trim, use decorative thread in the upper looper. We usually use larger beads and a heavier thread for this application. You must help feed the bead strand (gently) as you serge over it.

Beaded piping

To make a piping strip of beads or pearls, serge the strands to a folded 1-1/4"-wide strip of bias tricot or other lightweight fabric.

Applying sequins

To serge over sequin trim, the sequins must be narrow enough for the looper thread to lock over them. If you are applying them with a beading foot, they need to be less than 1/4" wide (see the previous instructions for applying beads and pearls). Place the trim so that the sequins overlap away from the presser foot. (Fig. 6-35) Serge over the sequin strand with a long stitch, being careful to avoid hitting the needle or knife. Use monofilament nylon thread or matching thread in the upper looper. After serging, slip the upper looper threads between the sequins so no thread is visible.

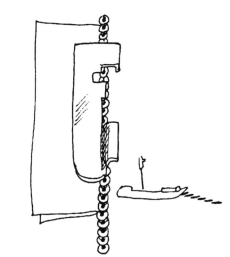

Fig. 6-35: Overlap sequin trim away from the presser foot.

Project: Beaded Victorian Sachets

Delight anyone on your gift list with a charming sachet covered by strands of pearls. (Fig. 6-36)

Fig. 6-36: Use these little pearl-studded sachet bags on a living-room table or in a lingerie drawer, or hang them from the Christmas tree.

Foot: Beading or no foot for bead application; standard for serge-seaming

Stitch: 3-thread

Stitch length: Medium—slightly longer than the individual bead for bead application; short for serge-seaming (to anchor the beads)

Stitch width: Narrow (use right needle for small pearls, left needle for medium pearls) to cover the bead; medium for serge-seaming

Thread: Matching color
  Needle: All-purpose or serger
  Upper looper: Monofilament nylon, all-purpose, or serger
  Lower looper: All-purpose or serger

Tension: Rolled edge for bead application; balanced for serge-seaming

Needle: Size 11/75

Fabric: 6" of 45"-wide taffeta; 6" of 45"-wide satin (for the lining)

Notions: 2 yards pearl beading; 1 yard satin cording (for the tie)

1. Cut one 7-1/2" by 6" rectangle from both the taffeta and satin.

2. Following the previous instructions, serge seven vertical rows of pearl beading to the taffeta rectangle. Begin and end 3/4" from the ends and space the rows 1" apart, as shown. (Fig. 6-37) Use a rolled-edge stitch and a beading foot, if available. Dab seam sealant on the ends of the pearl strands.

3. With the right sides of the satin lining and taffeta together, slowly straight-stitch the upper edge over the pearls. Use a 1/4" seam allowance and a short stitch length. Trim the beading ends.

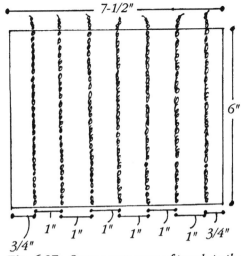

Fig. 6-37: *Serge seven rows of pearls to the right side of the taffeta rectangle.*

4. Find the midpoint of the cording and place it on the right side of the taffeta 1-1/2" down from the finished edge, as shown. (Fig. 6-38)

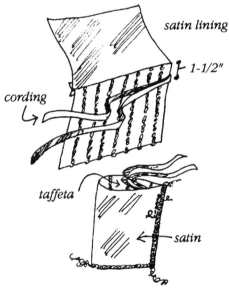

Fig. 6-38: *Place the middle of the cording on the right side of the taffeta and pearls. With the taffeta inside, serge-seam the bottom and side. Reinforce the cording ends with straight-stitching.*

5. Fold the satin and taffeta wrong sides together. Then fold the 6" ends together with the taffeta on the inside and the satin on the outside. Adjust for serge-seaming as specified. Serge-seam the lower and side edges with a 1/4" allowance. To secure the tie, straight-stitch across it along the serging needleline.

6. Turn the sachet right side out. Fill the bag with potpourri and tie it closed.

Lesson 29. Serging with Elastic Thread

In Lesson 18 we introduced decorative elasticized trims using clear elastic and elasticized binding with narrow braided elastic. Elastic thread can also be used decoratively.

Serge-covered cording

Elastic thread is widely available in white, but you can custom color it for button loops, ponytail bands, and package ties. Or braid several strands for straps or a headband.

1. For the best coverage, use woolly nylon thread in the upper looper of a short rolled-edge stitch. For the tightest stitch, also use woolly or monofilament nylon in the lower looper.

2. Place the elastic thread over the front and under the back of the presser foot, using the guidelines for serging over filler cord on page 48. Start with about 3" of elastic thread behind the foot. (Fig. 6-39)

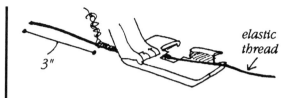

elastic thread

3"

Fig. 6-39: *Serge a woolly-nylon rolled edge over elastic thread to custom color it.*

3. Turn the flywheel a few times to begin forming stitches over the elastic. Then serge over the elastic, guiding it carefully between the needle and the knives. As you serge over it, hold the elastic taut from both ends, but do not stretch it.

Serged elastic button loops

Elastic thread may be used in the serger as well as for a filler cord. For anything from a baby garment to a delicate feminine effect, serge-finish an edge with elastic thread in the lower looper. Then simply pull out elastic button loops at desired intervals for a quick and easy decorative closure.

Because white elastic loops may not be suitable for all of your button-loop projects, you may want to purchase colored elastic thread. *Rainbow Elastic Plus* thread comes in a wide range of colors and in two weights. This colored elastic thread is available in many knitting stores and through mail-order sources.

1. Prepare your serger with decorative thread in the upper looper, elastic thread in the lower looper, and all-purpose or serger thread in the needle.

2. Adjust for a short, medium-width or wider stitch. We prefer the 3-thread, although a 3/4-thread stitch looks fine as well. Balance the tension with the upper looper thread slightly wrapping the edge. This makes the elastic invisible from the top side.

Special Tip: Because elastic thread stretches easily and because it can vary in weight, you might have to play with the lower looper (elastic thread) tension to get it adjusted properly. Even then, the lower looper thread loops probably will not be precisely even due to the nature of elastic thread. If you cannot loosen the lower looper tension enough, take the elastic thread out of the tension discs (see page 24).

3. After testing the stitch, serge-finish one side of the closure. For more stability, use the serge-a-fold technique on page 67.

4. Use pins to mark equidistant button placements along the outer edge of the serged elastic loops. With a fine crochet hook or tapestry needle, pull the elastic thread at each mark to form small, even loops. (Fig. 6-40) Pulling the elastic thread narrows and tightens the decorative edge slightly and anchors the loops.

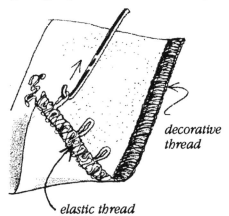

decorative thread

elastic thread

Fig. 6-40: *Serge-finish one edge with elastic thread in the lower looper. Pull the elastic to form loops.*

5. Serge the opposite edge with the same thread and settings.

Note: In some cases the pulling of the loops will significantly narrow the row of decorative stitching. If this happens, change to all-purpose or serger thread in the lower looper before serging the remaining edge. Readjust the stitch to match the width and appearance of the decorative serging on the looped edge.

6. Sew small buttons in the middle of the row of stitching opposite the elastic loops, matching the loop placements.

Project: Quick Baby Bib

Select a fun-print kitchen towel for this simple project. Use serged elastic button loops for the back closure. (Fig. 6-41)

Fig. 6-41: *Whip out several of these easy bibs for gifts or for your own beginning eater.*

Foot: Standard
Stitch: 3-thread
Stitch length: Short
Stitch width: Widest
Thread: Contrasting color
   Needle: All-purpose or serger
   Upper looper: Pearl cotton
   Lower looper: Elastic
Tension: Balanced
Needle: Size 11/75
Fabric: One kitchen towel with an
   appropriate print design
Notions: Four novelty buttons

1. Fold the towel in half lengthwise, then fold it in the opposite direction so one side is 4" shorter than the other. Mark the second fold as the shoulder line. (Fig. 6-42) The shorter end will be the back of the bib.

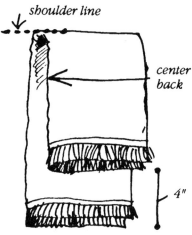

Fig. 6-42: *Fold the towel to mark the shoulder line.*

2. Using a children's pattern, cut a neckline edge, matching the shoulder-line mark to the pattern's shoulder seamline. (Fig. 6-43) Trim 3/8" of the seam allowance from the neckline and smooth out the curve if necessary. Cut along the center back for the bib opening.

3. Following the serge-a-fold technique, fold 1/4" to the underside along the right-side straight edge in the back. Straight-stitch along the fold.

4. Adjust your serger for serged elastic button loops and serge-finish the fold. End the serging at the fringe line.

5. Pull the elastic thread at equidistant intervals to form four button loops.

6. Serge-a-fold finish the other side of the opening to match, beginning at the fringe line.

7. Also using the serge-a-fold technique, finish the neckline edge. Lengthen the stitch slightly to avoid stretching the curved edge.

8. Trim the excess fabric next to the stitching on the underside of the bib. Thread all of the chain tails back through the stitching to secure. Attach buttons to match the loop placements.

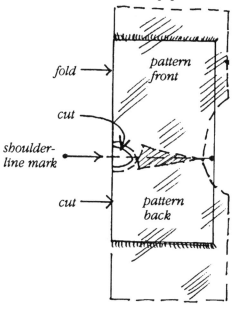

Fig. 6-43: *Overlap the pattern shoulder seam even with the shoulder-line mark. Cut the neckline edge and down the center back.*

7. Fabric Embellishment

In previous chapters we've discussed decorative seaming, edge-finishing, and special techniques. We've also included a number of brand-new serger applications that we discovered during our research for this book series. Double-bound seams and edges, clear elastic trim and piping, picot braid, tear-away braid, stretched couching braid, and serged elastic button loops are some notable examples.

In the final two chapters, we want to encourage you to explore, create, and discover new decorative possibilities with your serger.

Having the time to test and develop more ideas was the major factor limiting our research. Artistic possibilities seem endless—combinations of decorative techniques, unusual applications for existing techniques, and continuing exploration with new products and technology. What we have included in these last nine lessons is merely a starting point—for us and, we hope, for you—to push the serger to its creative limits.

Lesson 30. Heirloom Serging

Heirloom serging (a replication of French hand sewing) was an early example of serger-embellished fabric. Delicate rows of pintucks, lace inserts, serged trims and ribbon, and rolled edges can be applied quickly to a fabric such as batiste, organdy, or handkerchief linen. (Fig. 7-1) Beautiful heirloom serging is an art in itself.

Fig. 7-1: *Heirloom serging features dainty rows of pintucks, trim, and ribbon on lightweight fabric.*

You can embellish fabric using heirloom serging, or you may choose to construct a fancy band or trim that can be inserted into or top-stitched on top of your garment or project fabric.

Heirloom supplies

■ **Trims:** Lace, ribbon, entredeux, eyelet, embroidery, and beading. The lace may be insertion lace with two straight edges or edging lace with one scalloped edge. (You'll need at least one straight edge for serge-seaming the lace to the fabric.) (Fig. 7-2) Laces may be

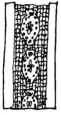

lace
insertion

lace
edging

ribbon   *entredeux*

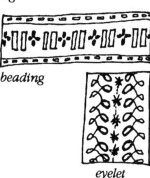

beading

embroidery

eyelet

Fig. 7-2: *A variety of trims are used in heirloom serging.*

either flat or ruffled, or you can gather flat lace using the methods in Lesson 23. Purchase trim wider than the presser foot for easiest serging. For narrower trim, flatlock or zigzag two or more strips side by side.

■ **Thread:** Lightweight—such as machine embroidery, metallic, or serger weight—to enhance the delicate look. Use woolly or monofilament nylon in the lower looper for the tightest rolled edges. You may also choose to use woolly nylon in the upper looper for maximum coverage.

■ **Needles:** New, sharp 11/75.

■ **Other supplies:** Spray starch; small, sharp scissors.

Heirloom design

One of the most difficult and time-consuming aspects of heirloom serging is the initial design because you have so many options. Build a straight-line design from the center out, working evenly on both sides of a center row.

Always embellish the fabric before cutting out a pattern. Add at least 2" additional length and width to your fabric requirements. Before serging, lay out the trim on the fabric. Put the pattern piece over the top to view the placement. For identical heirloom-serged pieces (two sleeves, for example), decorate twice the length rather than trying to duplicate the design side by side.

The easiest method for marking the trim placement lines is to serge each new row a presser foot's width from the previous one. For uneven spacing, you can press-mark the placement lines with your iron. Another option is to use an air-erasable marker, but test first to be sure the marking will disappear from your fabric.

Heirloom serging techniques

■ Attach trim using a narrow, satin-length, rolled-edge stitch. (As an option, a 2- or 3-thread flatlock can also be used.) The trim can be either serged on top of the fabric or inserted between fabric edges. The seams can be featured decoratively on the outside (our favorite) or pressed toward the fabric on the underside. (Fig. 7-3)

Seam allowances featured on outside:

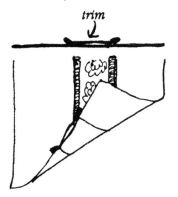

Seam allowances hidden on underside:

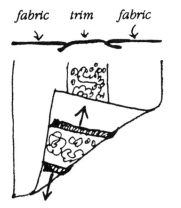

Fig. 7-3: *The trim can be pintuck-seamed on top of the fabric or inserted between it.*

■ Mark your needle stitching line on the presser foot if you haven't already. Align your seamline with this marking for the most accurate stitching. (Fig. 7-4)

■ Serge on the straight of grain of the fabric.

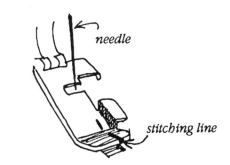

Fig. 7-4: *For accuracy, mark the needle stitching line on top of the foot.*

■ When inserting the trim strip, serge with wrong sides together to feature the stitching on the outside or with right sides together to hide it on the underside. (Fig. 7-5)

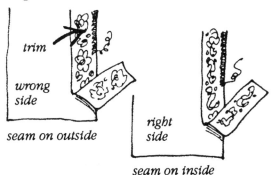

Fig. 7-5: *Always serge with the trim on top. Serge with wrong sides together to feature the seams on the outside, or with right sides together for hidden seams.*

■ When the ribbon or trim is layered on top of the fabric with decorative-tuck seams, fold the fabric with wrong sides together.

- When attaching an insertion trim or ribbon to the face of the fabric with a rolled-edge stitch, serge one long edge, turn the fabric, and serge from the opposite direction. (Fig. 7-6) The rolled edges will then always face out from the center trim.

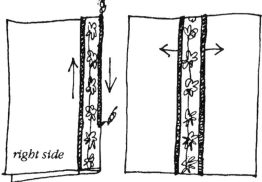

right side

Fig. 7-6: *For rolled edges to face outward from a trim, serge the two sides in opposite directions.*

- Add plain rows of rolled-edge tucks to enhance the design.

- When using a beading trim, thread narrow ribbon through the openings after it is attached.

- For a traditional heirloom look, press and spray-starch all of the fabric and lace before and after stitching. For a softer finish, press after serging each row, but don't use the spray starch.

Project: Heirloom Sampler Pillow

This keepsake pillow is a perfect accent for any bedroom. Delicate rows of heirloom serging belie the easy construction. (Fig. 7-7)

Fig. 7-7: *Apply heirloom serging to a piece of batiste before making a simple pillow.*

Foot: Rolled edge or standard for decorative (depending on model); standard for serge-seaming and serge-gathering
Stitch: 3-thread
Stitch length: Short for decorative; medium for serge-seaming and serge-gathering
Stitch width: Narrow for decorative; wide for serge-seaming and serge-gathering
Thread: Matching
  Needle: Serger
  Upper looper: Rayon for decorative; all-purpose or serger for serge-seaming and serge-gathering
  Lower looper: Monofilament or woolly nylon for decorative; all-purpose or serger for serge-seaming and serge-gathering
Tension: Rolled edge for decorative; balanced for serge-seaming and serge-gathering
Needle: Size 11/75
Fabric: 2/3 yard 45"-wide batiste or comparable
Notions: 3/8 yard polyester fleece; 1 package polyester fiberfill; 1 yard embroidered trim, at least 3/4" wide; 1-1/2 yards 3/4"-wide flat lace edging

1. From the fabric, cut two 3" by 45" strips for the ruffle and one 16" square for embellishing. Also cut one 12" circle of fabric for the pillow back and two 12-1/2" circles of fleece for the pillow. Use a plate or lid as a cutting guide.

2. Lightly press a crease line in the center of the 16" fabric square with wrong sides together. With one edge of the embroidered trim on the right-side edge of the crease, serge-seam the two together using the decorative settings specified.

3. Press, turn the fabric, and serge the other long edge of the trim to the fabric. Press again.

4. Using the width of the presser foot as a guide, serge a rolled-edge pintuck on both sides of the trim.

5. Press a crease line 1-1/2" from both tucks. Place the straight edge of the lace edging along the folds on the underside. Serge with the lace on top so the scalloped edge extends away from the center. (Fig. 7-8)

6. Press-mark a line 1" away from the scalloped edge of both lace strips.

7. Serge a rolled-edge tuck from the right side on both press-marks. Repeat two more tuck rows on either side, using the width of the presser foot as a measurement. Press the entire design carefully.

8. Cut a 12" circle from the embellished fabric, centering the embroidered trim.

9. Place the short ends of the ruffle strips together and serge-seam them into a circle using the rolled-edge stitch.

10. Decoratively serge-finish one long edge of the ruffle circle using the rolled-edge stitch.

11. Serge-gather the unfinished ruffle edge using one of the methods in Lesson 23.

12. Place the two fleece circles together and serge-seam, leaving a 4" opening.

13. Lightly stuff the fleece with fiberfill and serge-seam the opening closed, making the pillow form.

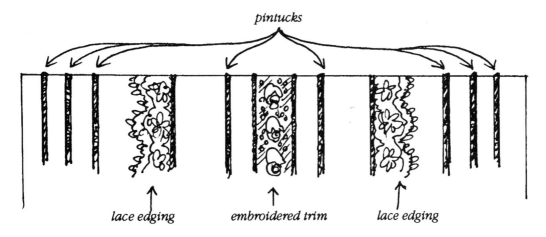

pintucks

lace edging   *embroidered trim*   *lace edging*

Fig. 7-8: *Use a simple heirloom design for a beginning project.*

14. With right sides together, place the ruffle on the embellished, pillow-top circle, matching the cut edges. Adjust the ruffle evenly. Serge-baste the ruffle to the fabric circle.

15. With the ruffle toward the center, serge the two pillow circles right sides together, leaving an 8" opening.

16. Turn the circles right side out and insert the fleece pillow form. Hand-stitch the opening closed.

Lesson 31. Ornamenting Fabric

In the last lesson, we used heirloom serging to ornament fabric. But you don't always have to use dainty stitches on lightweight woven fabrics in straight rows to embellish your fabric. Consider all of your ornamental serging possibilities. Most edge-finishes can be serged over folds, so you have the option of placing stitches anywhere on your fabric—and in any direction.

Try diagonal or vertical rows of corded rolled edges or flatlocking, perhaps to accent a stripe in the fabric. Test parallel rows of wide, balanced, satin serging to duplicate current designer fabrics. (Or try prepleating a fabric with a *Perfect Pleater* device and serge-finishing each tuck.) Consider serging with uneven spacing, sporadically placed stitching, or combinations of techniques. (Fig. 7-9)

The 2-thread double chainstitch (see page 6) can also be used to serge a design or a random pattern on the fabric. Remove the presser foot and hold the fabric taut while serging.

Experiment with all fabric types and any decorative thread. Test ideas from ready-to-wear. Let your imagination soar. We include a few test results here, but these are only the beginning. There's plenty of room for innovation in serger sewing. Have fun, experiment, and let us know what you discover.

Chain-loop serging

Our first idea for chain-loop serging was to serge on and off a fold or edge, using a satin rolled edge and leaving thread-chain loops at intervals along the stitching. We serged for a distance and then chained off the fabric. To form a loop, we raised the presser foot, an-

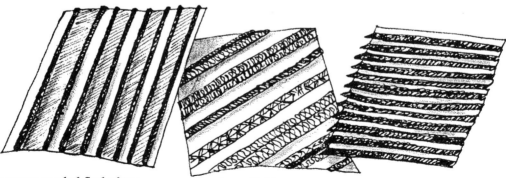

narrow corded flatlocking   random stitching   serged pleats

Fig. 7-9: *Ornament fabrics with corded flatlocking on stripes, random diagonal stitches, or narrow serged pleats.*

chored the needle right where the chain left the fabric, and began serging again.

Although we achieved an interesting effect, the method was slow and tedious. We discovered a faster, more random effect by raising the front of the presser foot only to insert the fabric. We were also successful in serging with the presser foot removed the entire time, chaining off and on easily. Leave the chain in loops or cut it at varying lengths. Don't worry if you cut the fabric while serging, because the rolled edge covers any cuts. (Fig. 7-10)

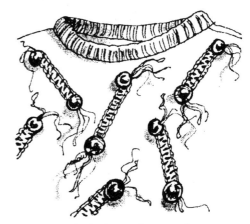

Fig. 7-11: *Flatlock random patches on your fabric. Tie beads onto the tails.*

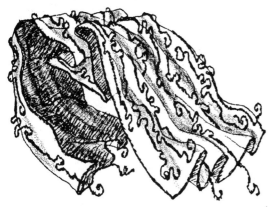

Fig. 7-10: *Use chain-loop serging to embellish a piece of fabric or a finished scarf.*

Flatlocked patches

With a heavier thread such as pearl rayon in the upper looper, create short patches of flatlocking in the middle of your fabric, leaving thread tails at each end. Tie beads onto the tails for an added ornamental touch. (Fig. 7-11) Mark the placement of your flatlocked patches or apply them randomly. Fold along the placement line. Remove the stitches from the stitch finger and pull out about 3" of unchained thread. Raise the presser foot and anchor the needle at the end of the placement line.

Flatlock the patch, lift the presser foot, remove the stitches from the stitch finger, and pull the threads away from the serging. Do not chain off. Knot the threads at each end or attach beads to secure the stitching. If you prefer, pull the thread ends through to the wrong side of the fabric for securing.

Try decorative patches using a rolled-edge or narrow, balanced stitch. Or try chaining on and off the fabric for a different effect.

Finger tensioning

We used finger tensioning on the needle thread to gather lightweight fabric in Lesson 23 (page 110). It also can be used to vary the look of your decorative stitching.

Try applying tension on the looper threads in the same manner. On some machines, we found that we could create a variety of interesting effects. With a satin-length, medium-width, balanced stitch and a rolled-edge setting, we used

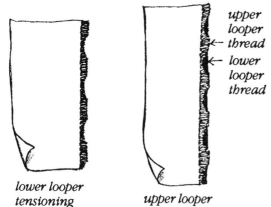

lower looper
tensioning

upper looper
tensioning

upper
looper
← thread
← lower
looper
thread

Fig. 7-12: *Use lower looper tensioning to create a scalloped rolled edge. Or try upper looper tensioning for a scalloped pattern on top of the stitching.*

lower looper tensioning to create a delicately scalloped edge. (Fig. 7-12)

Using **upper looper tensioning,** we created an unusual scalloped pattern on the top side of a balanced satin stitch. The pattern worked best in our testing using a satin-length, 4mm-width, balanced stitch and the standard presser foot. With contrasting thread colors in the loopers, we applied upper-looper finger tensioning at regular intervals to form the pattern.

On other models, we've tried applying tension to the looper threads with little success. We then went back to the needle thread (used for tension gathering). By putting tension on the needle thread of a narrow flatlock at equal intervals, we achieved a scalloped flatlocked effect. (Fig. 7-13)

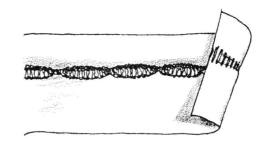

Fig. 7-13: *Use needle-thread finger tensioning for a scalloped flatlock.*

Experiment with finger tensioning on all of your threads. Results can vary from machine to machine. Try using rolled-edge, flatlock, and balanced stitching. Test with different threads, stitch widths, and lengths.

Serge-and-sew stitching

Use some of the optional decorative stitches on your sewing machine in combination with decorative serging. Select contrasting thread for the serging and sewing. The serging thread must be heavy enough to form an attractive satin stitch and the sewing thread must fit through the eye of the needle.

Flatlock rows, either parallel or at random, on your project fabric following the instructions in Lessons 3 and 25. Use a decorative thread in the upper looper and flatlock over folds with the fabric wrong sides together.

With your sewing machine, sew ornamental stitches directly on top of and/or right next to the flatlocked rows. (Fig. 7-14) You may need to hold the

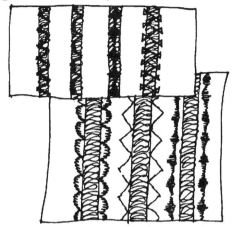

Fig. 7-14: *Place a fancy sewing-machine stitch over or next to flatlocking to create serge-and-sew stitching.*

serged thread chain behind the presser foot to begin sewing over it smoothly. If you need more thread coverage in the ornamental stitch, loosen the sewing machine's needle tension.

For a wider serge-and-sew stitch, use a double flatlock. (Fig. 7-15) Fold the

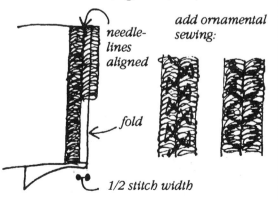

Fig. 7-15: *Serge a double flatlock for wider serge-and-sew embellishment.*

fabric parallel to a single row of flatlocking, half a stitch width away. Flatlock over the fold matching the needlelines, pull the stitches flat, and sew an ornamental stitch on top.

If your rows of serge-and-sew stitching will be crossing each other (see our coaster project, following), first flatlock all the rows in one direction. Then add the ornamental stitching before completing the rows in the opposite direction.

Project: Serge-and-Sew Coasters

These speedy coasters proclaim both your sewing and serging skills. Make a set of four, or double the project for a set of eight. (Fig. 7-16)

Fig. 7-16: *Serge-and-sew coasters are much easier to make than they appear.*

Foot: Standard
Stitch: 3-thread
Stitch length: Short
Stitch width: Widest
Thread: Contrasting color; buttonhole twist for sewing machine
Needle: All-purpose or serger
Upper looper: Cotton crochet

Lower looper: All-purpose or serger
for flatlocking; cotton crochet for
serge-finishing
Tension: Flatlock for decorative;
balanced for serge-finishing
Needle: Size 11/75
Fabric: 1/4 yard cotton or cotton/
polyester
Notions: 1/4 yard heavy fusible
interfacing; 1/4 yard polyester
fleece; 1/2 yard paper-backed
fusible web

1. Fuse the interfacing to the back of
half the fabric.

2. Flatlock diagonal rows across the
interfaced fabric, approximately 1-1/4"
apart.

3. Stitch over the flatlocked rows using
an ornamental sewing machine stitch.
Choose a serpentine stitch or a multiple
zigzag to flatten the flatlocking as much
as possible (because you'll be serging
over it in the next step).

4. Flatlock equidistant rows in the
opposite direction and add the decorative sewing-machine stitching on top.

5. Using the fusible web, fuse the fleece
to the back of the embellished fabric.
Then fuse the remaining fabric to the
fleece.

6. Cut four 4" squares from the layered
fabric.

7. Using a short, balanced stitch, serge-
finish the coaster edges. Dab the corners
with seam sealant and clip the thread
chains when dry.

Lesson 32.
Serger Cutwork

When serger cutwork was first introduced by Sue Green-Baker in 1988, we
thought it was a fascinating technique. It
took considerable skill and patience,
though, because we needed to serge-
finish the inner edges of small holes cut
in a piece of fabric. (Fig. 7-17)

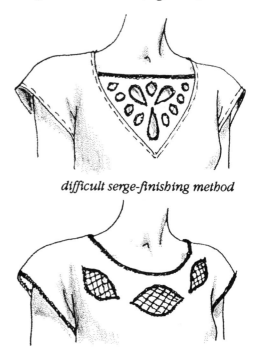

difficult serge-finishing method

easy water-soluble-stabilizer method

Fig. 7-17: *Serger cutwork options.*

Then we discovered an interesting
new product—water-soluble stabilizer—
and started experimenting. The results
were a speedy combination of sewing
and serging that created an interesting
new appliquéd cutwork.

This newer method works equally well
for garments, table linens, and craft

projects. The cutwork appliqué must be applied to a washable fabric because the washable stabilizer has to be dissolved in water to complete the project.

Serging over the stabilizer gives the stitches a stiff, starched effect. Test various threads and stitch types for the desired look. For example, woolly nylon in a satin rolled edge creates a stiff design. With a longer, balanced stitch, woolly nylon gives a softer appearance.

1. With a water-soluble pen, draw a cutwork design outline on the project fabric. (Fig. 7-18)

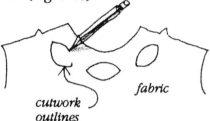

cutwork
outlines

fabric

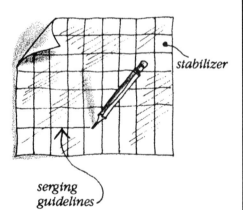

stabilizer

serging
guidelines

Fig. 7-18: *Draw cutwork outlines on the fabric and serging guidelines on the water-soluble stabilizer.*

2. Cut a piece of water-soluble stabilizer larger than the design on all sides. Allow an extra 1/4" for each line of serging you will be applying, then add an additional inch on each side of the piece.

3. Draw serging guidelines onto the stabilizer. (Fig. 7-18) For more durability, draw the guidelines close together and limit the size of the appliqué. Plan straight rows of serging for your first project—serging a curved fold can be tricky.

 Optional: For a quick project, don't bother to draw guidelines. Just serge parallel rows a presser-foot width apart, using the foot as a guide.

4. Fold the stabilizer on the guidelines and serge over the folds with a stitch adjustment you have previously tested. (Don't worry if you cut the stabilizer.)

5. Place the decorated stabilizer over the design outline on the right side of the base fabric. Use an embroidery hoop to align the two layers and hold them flat. (Fig. 7-19) Be sure the serged stitches extend past the design outline on all sides.

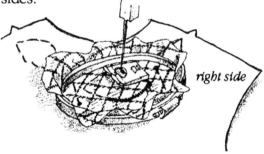

right side

Fig. 7-19: *Align the serged stabilizer over the cutwork outline using an embroidery hoop. Zigzag the stitched stabilizer to the fabric.*

6. With matching thread and a narrow satin stitch, zigzag the stabilizer to the fabric following the design outline.

7. Remove the hoop and carefully trim the stabilizer close to the outside of the zigzag stitch. Then trim away the fabric from behind the stabilizer appliqué. Be

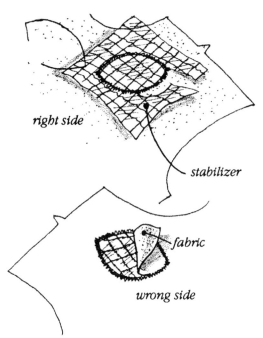

right side

stabilizer

fabric

wrong side

Fig. 7-20: *Trim the stabilizer outside the zigzagging on the front. Trim the fabric inside the zigzagging on the back.*

careful not to cut the zigzag stitch or the fabric. (Fig. 7-20)

8. Place an unembellished piece of water-soluble stabilizer over the right side of the appliqué and secure both layers in the embroidery hoop. To finish and secure the cutwork, stitch through the stabilizer over the original zigzagging. Use a satin-length, zigzag stitch a little wider than the original stitching in step 6.

9. Trim away the stabilizer from both sides of the stitching, then submerge the cutwork appliqué in water to remove the excess. Allow the project to air-dry, or press it dry between two press cloths.

Project: Convenient Stationery Organizer

Correspondence and thank-you notes are right at hand in this specially designed folder. The cutwork design adds a loving sentiment. (Fig. 7-21)

Fig. 7-21: *Organize your stationery or serge a special gift for a friend.*

Foot: Rolled edge or standard for cutwork (depending on model); standard for serge-finishing
Stitch: 3-thread
Stitch length: Short
Stitch width: Narrow for cutwork; widest for serge-finishing
Thread: Matching for cutwork; contrasting for serge-finishing
 Needle: All-purpose or serger
 Upper looper: All-purpose or serger for cutwork; pearl rayon or buttonhole twist for serge-finishing
 Lower looper: All-purpose or serger for cutwork; pearl rayon or buttonhole twist for serge-finishing
Tension: Rolled edge for cutwork; balanced for serge-finishing
Needle: Size 11/75 for cutwork; size 14/90 for serge-finishing
Fabric: 1/2 yard taffeta or comparable; 1/4 yard batiste or comparable

Notions: Two 6" by 6" squares water-soluble stabilizer; air-erasable or water-soluble marker; 1/2 yard fleece; 1-1/3 yard paper-backed, fusible transfer web; 1/2 yard 3/8"-wide ribbon; one letter-sized file folder

1. Cut two 18" by 12" rectangles each of taffeta and fleece plus four of fusible web. Cut one 18" by 6" rectangle and one 7-1/2" by 4" rectangle for pockets. With the file folder closed, trim it to 8-1/2" deep, cutting off the tab and leaving the width the same.

2. Using the marker, draw a cutwork pattern on the batiste, following the pattern grid. (Fig. 7-22)

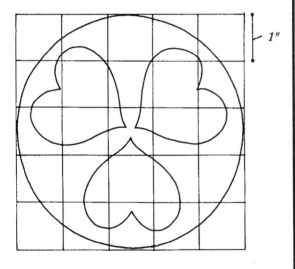

Fig. 7-22: Heart cutwork pattern grid.

3. Serge one stablizer sheet with rows of stitching in a crisscrossed design of your choice. Extend the rows of serging to fill the stabilizer square.

4. Center the serged stabilizer over the cutwork pattern and apply it to the batiste following the previous instructions.

5. Using a saucer or lid as a guide, draw a 6" circle with the cutwork centered inside. With the same stitch used for the cutwork, serge a rolled edge on the circular line.

6. Top-stitch the cutwork appliqué to the right side of one taffeta rectangle, centered over one half (which will become the front of the organizer).

7. Fuse the wrong side of both fabric rectangles to a fleece rectangle.

8. Using the serge-finishing settings specified and the serge-a-fold technique from page 67, decoratively serge one long edge of both pocket rectangles.

9. Place the larger pocket along the lower edge of the taffeta rectangle without the cutwork, matching the cut edges. Layer the smaller pocket over it in the lower-right corner, also matching the cut edges. (Fig. 7-23) Top-stitch vertically through the center of the larger pocket and finish the left side of the smaller pocket by turning under 1/2" and top-stitching.

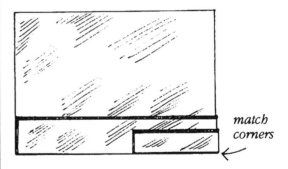

match corners

Fig. 7-23: Layer the pocket pieces, with the serged folds up, over the inside organizer piece.

10. Straight-stitch two rows 1" apart next to the small pocket to hold a pen.

11. Fuse the fleece side of both rectangles to opposite sides of the file folder, matching all cut edges. Using the saucer or lid as a guide, round all four corners.

12. Cut the ribbon into two equal lengths. Center and pin one piece each on both opening edges of the folder. Starting at the center of the lower edge, decoratively serge-finish the outer organizer edge, being careful not to hit the pins. Apply a dab of seam sealant where the stitching crosses and trim the thread chain when dry.

Lesson 33.
Serged Appliqué

Appliqué is one of our favorite embellishments because it offers so many options for creativity. You can use it to add texture, color, and a three-dimensional effect to any fabric. Fashion your own design to adorn your latest garments, sweaters, accessories, or home decoration projects.

In the past, we've worked with flat and 3-D appliqué. We've also tried padded appliqué. Just about any serged edge-finish or trim can be used. Other techniques such as serger lace and serging over sequins, beads, or pearls adapt well to appliqué. Let your creativity guide you.

Serge-finish the edges of the pieces you plan to appliqué. A satin rolled-edge stitch is the most common for edge finishing, but any serged edge is possible.

Apply the appliqué pieces to your fabric by top-stitching all of the edges flat, top-stitching only part of the edges (for a raised or 3-D appliqué), or attaching them by hand-tacking, fusing, or fabric painting. (Fig. 7-24)

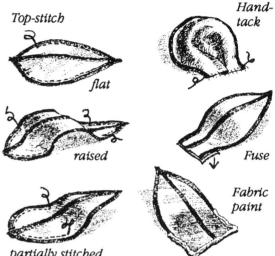

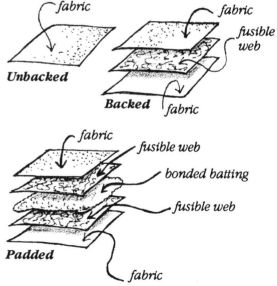

Fig. 7-24: *Appliqué serge-finished pieces to your project fabric.*

Appliqués may be unbacked, backed, or padded. (Fig. 7-25) Unbacked

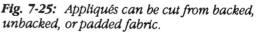

Fig. 7-25: *Appliqués can be cut from backed, unbacked, or padded fabric.*

appliqués are usually applied flat to the project fabric with the underside of the appliqué fabric hidden. Make backed appliqués simply by sandwiching a layer of fusible transfer web between two layers of fabric (right sides out) so that both sides of the appliqué will appear finished when they are applied by the raised or 3-D methods.

Make padded appliqués by sandwiching bonded batting between two layers of fusible transfer web. Then fuse the batting and web between two layers of fabric, with the web against the wrong side of the fabric. Padded appliqués are most often applied raised or 3-D, in the same manner as unpadded, backed appliqués.

Project: Appliquéd Dusting Mitt

Get your house squeaky clean with this washable dusting mitt. It's simple to make and takes some of the drudgery out of a less-than-favorite household task. (Fig. 7-26)

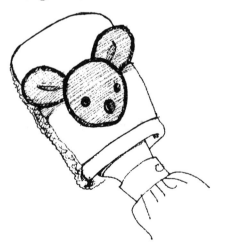

Fig. 7-26: *A perky mouse keeps you company as you do your dusting.*

Foot: Rolled edge or standard for appliqué (depending on model); standard for serge-seaming
Stitch: 3-thread
Stitch length: Short for appliqué; medium for serge-seaming
Stitch width: Narrow for appliqué; wide for serge-seaming
Thread: Contrasting color for appliqué; matching for serge-seaming
Needle: All-purpose or serger
Upper looper: Crochet for appliqué; all-purpose or serger for serge-seaming
Lower looper: Woolly or monofilament nylon for appliqué; all-purpose or serger for serge-seaming
Tension: Rolled edge for appliqué; balanced for serge-seaming
Needle: Size 14/90
Fabric: 1/4 yard robe velour for mitt front; 1/6 yard of contrasting-color robe velour for appliqué; 1/4 yard cotton terry for mitt back and lining
Notions: One 6" square polyester fleece; 1/6 yard paper-backed fusible web; two 5/8" buttons; one 7/8" button

1. Cut one 9-1/2" by 6-1/2" velour rectangle for the mitt front and three 9-1/2" by 6-1/2" terry rectangles.

2. Fuse the fleece to one edge on the back of the appliqué fabric. Then fuse more fusible web to the back of the fleece. Next to that, fuse an 8" by 4" rectangle of fusible web. Remove the paper backing and, with wrong sides together, fuse the 8" by 4" rectangle to the rest of the unfinished appliqué fabric.

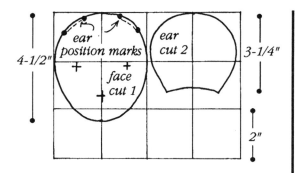

Fig. 7-27: *Mouse appliqué pattern grid.*

3. From the padded piece, cut the head using the grid shown. (Fig. 7-27) Cut the ears from the fused fabric.

4. With the appliqué settings specified, serge-finish the head, overlapping the stitching at the lower edge. Serge-finish the curved part of the ears.

5. Pleat the ears and pin the raw edges 1/2" under the head, as shown. (Fig. 7-28) Fuse the head to the right side of

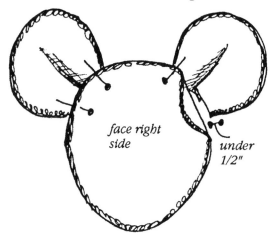

Fig. 7-28: *Pleat the ears and pin the raw edges into position.*

the mitt front. Top-stitch around the head on the serging needleline, catching the lower edge of the ears in the stitching.

6. Round the upper two corners of all the rectangles. Pin the ears back over the face until you finish serge-seaming. With the mitt front and one terry rectangle right sides together, serge-seam around the sides and top. Repeat for the other two terry rectangles.

7. Turn the appliquéd portion right side out and slip it over the other portion, with the wrong sides of the two portions together. (Fig. 7-29)

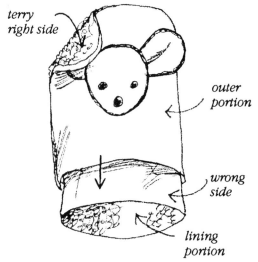

Fig. 7-29: *Slide the outside of the mitt, right side out, over the mitt lining portion.*

8. Matching the seams and cut edges, serge-finish the lower edge. Turn a 3/4" hem to the wrong side and top-stitch it in place.

Lesson 34.
Constructing Fabric

So far in this chapter, we've discussed ways of embellishing fabric with heirloom serging, cutwork, and appliqué. We've also outlined several other ways of ornamenting your fabric with serged stitches. Now we want to consider ways of using the serger to actually construct fabric for your project.

Serged piecing

Myriad pieced designs are possible by mixing fabric types, textures, or colors to complement the design of your garment or project. The method of seaming the elements together can be decorative as well. Exposed seams of any type or color are an option, and they can be serged more quickly than with a sewing machine because of the serger's faster stitching.

Serged patchwork, explored in depth by quilting professionals, is one piecing application. But there are some very different pieced looks now popular in ready-to-wear. Called mixed media, a variety of fabrics in random shapes are combined in one garment. (Fig. 7-30) Just about everything is being mixed these days, so be daring!

Always piece the fabric before cutting out the pattern. As with heirloom serging, the most time-consuming part of piecing is to determine the design. You may want to sketch the finished project with fabric design lines before cutting or even purchasing the fabrics.

Piecing is an excellent way to use smaller pieces or scraps of the more expensive fabric you have on hand (such as real and synthetic leathers and suedes,

Fig. 7-30: *For a mixed-media effect, decoratively serge together sections of different fabrics.*

fine wools, and silks), so try to work these into your designs as well. When cutting out the pieces, be sure to include 1/4" serging seam allowances on all sides of every piece.

If your serged seams will be inside rather than decoratively exposed, serge with the widest, 3- or 3/4-thread, balanced stitch. Plan your seaming strategy so that you serge smaller pieces into larger ones and then join the larger ones

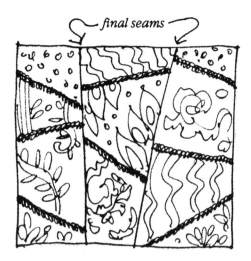

Fig. 7-31: *Serge-seam smaller pieces into larger ones. Then join the larger pieces.*

Fig. 7-32: *Serge in an insert of a different fabric before cutting out your project.*

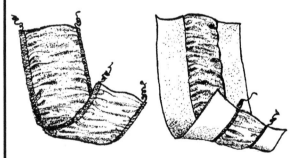

Fig. 7-33: *Serge-gather a fabric strip and insert into your yardage.*

together. (Fig. 7-31) When your piecing is at right angles, serge on the lengthwise grain first and then on the crosswise. If the design is diagonal, be sure to keep all lengthwise grainlines perpendicular (except for skins or synthetic suedes and leather, which may be cut in any direction).

Serged inserts and puffing

Inserts are actually a simple form of fabric piecing. In heirloom serging, one option is to stitch a lace insertion into the design. But inserts can be entirely different than heirloom lace. Strips of synthetic suede or leather can be placed strategically in the middle of your fashion fabric. Tapestry inserts add a hand-detailed effect. Adding a woven band to a knit fabric is another popular insert option. (Fig. 7-32)

With lighter-weight fabric, you can serge-gather both long edges of a strip and insert it as a decorative detail. (Fig. 7-33) This technique is called puffing. It is seen in everything from activewear jogging suits to delicate heirloom dresses.

Weaving serged strips

Weave together serge-finished strips to create another interesting ornamental fabric. (Fig. 7-34) By weaving the strips over fusible interfacing, the strips are held neatly in place.

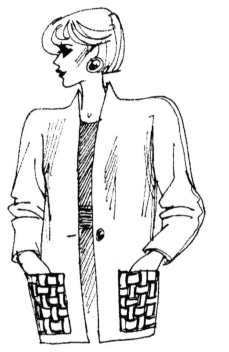

Fig. 7-34: *Weave and fuse serge-finished strips to create fabric.*

Any fabric can be used for weaving. For variety, use different fabrics or strip widths in the same design. If the fabric is unstable (a knit, for example), cut the strip twice the desired finished width, press in half lengthwise with wrong sides together, and serge-finish the edges double layer. For even more stability, fuse the layers together before serge-finishing.

Use any thread or stitch to serge-finish the strip edges. We like the coverage of woolly nylon and a narrow balanced stitch. Use decorative thread in the upper looper and matching all-purpose or serger thread in the needle and lower looper.

1. Cut a square of woven or knit fusible interfacing 2" larger on all sides than the finished size of the woven design.

2. With the fusible side up, place the longer strips right side up on the interfacing with the long edges butted together. Lightly fuse-baste the short edges to the interfacing on one end.

3. Weave shorter strips through the longer strips for several rows. Reposition them at right angles and butt the edges before fuse-basting to secure. (Fig. 7-35)

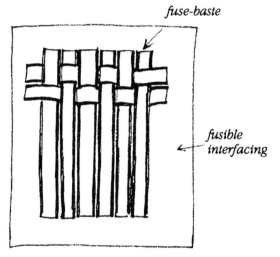

Fig. 7-35: *Fuse-baste one end of the longer strips. Weave the shorter strips through, fuse-basting periodically.*

4. Continue intermittently weaving and fuse-basting for the remainder of the rows.

5. After the weaving is completed, fuse securely. Cut the pattern from the woven fabric. The strips may then be top-stitched to the interfacing, if desired, for more durability.

6. Secure the ends of the woven strips in a seam or serge-finish them. When serging over the woven fabric in a straight line, follow a strip edge to keep the design uniform.

Project: Woven Pencil Case

This serged-strip pencil case is a great gift for your favorite student or business person. Select fabrics and decorative edging to suit any taste. (Fig. 7-36)

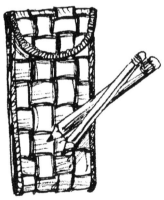

Fig. 7-36: *Woven serge-finished strips make the fabric for a quick and easy pencil case.*

Foot: Standard
Stitch: 3-thread
Stitch length: Short
Stitch width: Narrow for strip finish-
    ing; wide for serge-finishing
Thread: Contrasting color
    Needle: All-purpose or serger

Upper looper: Woolly nylon
Lower looper: Woolly nylon
Tension: Balanced
Needle: Size 14/90
Fabric: 2/3 yard denim
Notions: 2/3 yard fusible knit interfac-
    ing (or a 5" by 22" rectangle); 3/4" of
    3/4"-wide *Velcro*

1. Cut nine 1" by 20" strips of the denim and a 5" by 22" rectangle of the interfacing.

2. Serge-finish the long edges of all the strips.

3. Using five of the nine strips, cut twenty 5"-long sections.

4. Place the wrong side of the long strips side by side on top of the fusible side of the interfacing. Fuse-baste the upper end to anchor them.

5. Starting at the upper end, weave the shorter strips through the longer ones. Align and fuse-baste the strips after every three.

6. Continue until all the strips are woven. Steam and fuse well.

7. Round the upper edge of the woven piece.

8. Serge-finish the lower edge of the piece. Then serge-finish around the sides and curved top, directly over the long outer edges.

9. Center and top-stitch the hooked side of the *Velcro* 1-1/2" from the lower edge on the right side of the woven piece.

10. Center and top-stitch the looped *Velcro* piece on the underside of the curved edge to match.

11. Fold up the lower edge 7-1/2". Straight-stitch along the matched needlelines on the sides to complete the case.

8. Serger Chain Art

- **Lesson 35. Thread-Chain Cording**
- **Lesson 36. Thread-Chain Fringe**
- **Lesson 37. Thread-Chain Tassels**
- **Lesson 38. Thread-Chain Jewelry**

Our varied uses for serger thread-chain developed gradually over a period of years, working with and writing about serging. We began by using the chain for professional-looking button and belt loops and progressed from there.

Since our first two books (*Distinctive Serger Gifts & Crafts* and *Simply Serge Any Fabric*), we have experimented with additional thread-chain uses. Others have, too. In fact, some creative individuals are beginning to explore "serger art." We continue to marvel at how such a practical machine can be used in so many exciting ways.

One major medium for serger artistry is serger thread chain. With the wide array of decorative threads and yarns available for serger use, possibilities abound for interesting thread-chain projects. And the speedy serger can make yards and yards of chain in minimal time.

We've been experimenting with thread-chain cording, fringe, tassels, and jewelry. (Fig. 8-1) Thread-chain projects are suitable for everything from crafts and home decoration to accessories and your latest fashion garments. Plus, you won't have to worry about not finding the perfect color or texture—you can coordinate it yourself.

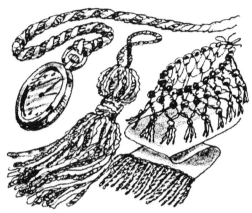

Fig. 8-1: *Artistic uses for serger chain include cording, tassels, fringe, and jewelry.*

To make a conventional serger thread chain:

1. Remove the presser foot and adjust your machine for a rolled-edge stitch.

2. Put the thread, yarn, or ribbon you want to feature in the upper looper. This thread will be the most visible in the chain. Anything you can serge with is possible. Try ribbon floss, fine yarn, or any decorative thread.

3. Thread the needle with a lightweight matching or monofilament nylon thread. This thread will be the least visible in the chain. For variety, test other lightweight threads. Fine metallic thread adds a sparkly touch, while top-stitching thread changes the texture or color.

4. Use woolly or monofilament nylon in the lower looper for the tightest rolled-edge stitch and the firmest chain. Tighten the lower looper tension as much as possible when using shiny thread such as rayon in the upper looper.

S **Special Tip:** You may find it impossible to form a tightly rolled edge with a slippery thread in the upper looper. If so, try instead to make a flatter chain by tightening the upper looper tension, too, for a more balanced stitch. (Fig. 8-2)

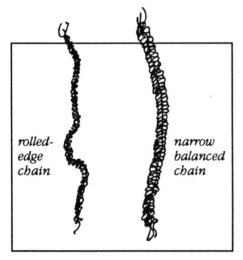

rolled-edge chain

narrow balanced chain

Fig. 8-2: *In a rolled-edge thread chain, both the needle and lower looper threads form a straight line. When the stitch is more balanced, the chain is flatter.*

5. Adjust your stitch length and tensions for the thread you're using. When using heavy thread such as pearl cotton or crochet thread, start with a medium stitch length and shorten it gradually to get the most attractive stitch formation. If the stitch length is too short, heavy thread can jam at the presser foot.

6. Hold the thread chain taut for a more uniform chain. If there are skipped stitches in the chain, try switching to a size 14/90 needle. Also try loosening the tensions a small amount, one at a time. First adjust the lower looper, then the upper looper, and finally the needle.

Test unusual thread-chain stitching options. Vary the stitch size and tensions. Try serging over one or more strands of heavy filler. Or, substitute fine wire for the filler cord. (We'll use fine wire as a filler later in this lesson to wrap a tassel.) Puffed serged braid (page 98) is actually a thread-chain variation made with balanced tension and a thicker filler.

Thread chain can also be serged over elastic cording (see Lesson 29, page 132). This stretchable, serge-covered cord works nicely for stringing necklaces and bracelets.

Lesson 35. Thread-Chain Cording

Make cording from serger thread chain by using the bobbin winder on your sewing machine. For heavier cording, make thread chain using decorative thread in both loopers and serge over a filler or use more strands of chain in the cording.

Fig. 8-3: *Attach serged chain strands to the bobbin and wind. Hold the cording at the halfway point and wind the outer half back onto the bobbin half.*

1. Knot one or more long strands of thread chain through a hole in the bobbin. (Fig. 8-3) The strand(s) should be about three times as long as the desired cording length. The length of the strand is limited by the length of your arms, unless you have one person run the machine while another holds the chain.

S **Special Tip:** If your bobbin doesn't have a hole on top to feed the cord through, put the cord through the center hole of the bobbin before putting it on the bobbin winder. If there is too much bulk for the

bobbin to sit on the winder securely, tie a piece of lightweight textured yarn (such as mohair) to the chain and feed the yarn through the center bobbin hole. This technique also works well if you are using heavier chain or more strands than can be attached to the bobbin at one time.

2. Hold the free end of the chain securely. Wind the bobbin until the strands are firmly twisted.

3. Before removing the cording from the bobbin, hold the twisted strands at the halfway point with your other hand. The cording will automatically twist back on itself. Pull the cording until the twisting is uniform.

Thread-chain cording may be used for decorative accents (such as edge trimming or couching), accessory items (necklaces or belts), or home decoration (pillow trims and drapery tie-backs).

Floating cording

If your cording is narrow enough, you can flatlock over it to attach it to fabric. For larger cording, or if you choose to knot it or string beads onto it, flatlocking over the cording isn't an option. To prevent having to tediously hand-tack the cording, thread it through a floating flatlock stitch instead.

1. Using the widest, longest flatlock setting and monofilament nylon thread in the needle, flatlock the fabric with right sides together.

2. Trim one end of the cording at an angle, saturate it with seam sealant, and roll it into a point. When dry, the cord-

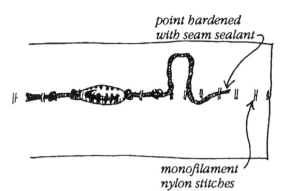

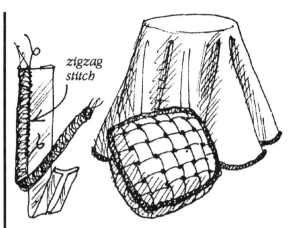

Fig. 8-4: *Float cording on top of the fabric by threading it under the ladder side of a flatlock.*

Fig. 8-5: *Make jumbo piping by zigzagging cording to a bias strip.*

ing can be easily threaded under the ladder stitches of the flatlock. (Fig. 8-4)

3. Make knots or bows in the cording or string on beads as you thread it through. You don't need to thread the cording through every stitch, but it's best to anchor it under a stitch just before and after each knot or bead.

4. Catch the cording ends in a seam, or hand-tack them to secure.

Jumbo corded piping

Corded piping was made in Lesson 14 by serging over a filler cord onto a piping strip. When the cording is too large to serge over, however, this method will not work. Instead, use bias tape to make a jumbo corded piping, popular for insertion into seams of pillows and slipcovers or to edge a tablecloth.

1. Make thread-chain cording using a heavy decorative thread and filler, following the previous instructions.

2. Using 1"-wide, single-fold bias tape in a matching or blending color, butt the cording against one long edge of the tape. (Fig. 8-5)

3. Use your sewing machine with a wide zigzag, matching thread, and a zipper foot to sew the cording to the tape.

Project: Simple Corded Wrap

Show off your serger cording in a versatile accessory. Use this practical wrap either as a tie belt or a long necklace. (Fig. 8-6)

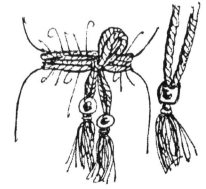

Fig. 8-6: *Two lengths of thread-chain cording and two large beads quickly combine for an attractive belt or necklace.*

Foot: Removed
Stitch: 3-thread
Stitch length: Short
Stitch width: Any
Thread: Any color
  Needle: All-purpose or serger
  Upper looper: Decorative
  Lower looper: Decorative
Tension: Rolled edge
Needle: Size 11/75
Notions: Decorative thread for filler;
  two large-eyed beads

1. Serge 48 yards of thread chain over matching filler.

2. Cut the chain into twelve 4-yard sections.

3. Make two 6-strand lengths of cording using the previous instructions. Both should be about 48" long.

4. Place the two lengths of cording side by side. Wrap one end tightly with cellophane tape for easy threading, then put both beads onto the double strand of cording. (Fig. 8-7)

Fig. 8-7: Wrap cellophane tape around one end of both strands and thread them together through the two beads before knotting the ends.

5. Tie knots about 4" from each end and separate the thread chains to make fringe. Slip one bead to each side. Secure the thread-chain ends with seam sealant and trim evenly when dry.

Lesson 36. Thread-Chain Fringe

Make decorative fringe from serger thread chain to coordinate with any project. Use thread in the chain that will hang limply and allow the fringe to swing freely with movement. Simply wrap the chain around tear-away stabilizer, serge-finish one long edge, clip open the opposite edge, and tear away the stabilizer.

1. For 1" fringe, cut a piece of tear-away stabilizer 3" wide by the desired length. Fold it lengthwise into a 1" width (three layers). Vary the width of the stabilizer strip to change the depth of the fringe.

2. Loosely wrap the chain around the stabilizer.

3. With a wide, satin-length, balanced stitch, serge along one edge with the same decorative thread in the upper looper. (Fig. 8-8)

tear-away stabilizer layers

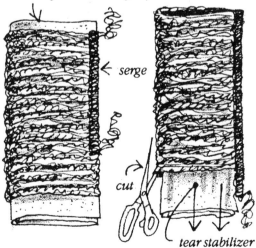

serge

cut

tear stabilizer

Fig. 8-8: Wrap the chain around the stabilizer. Serge the upper edge and cut the lower edge. Tear away the stabilizer for the finished fringe.

4. Dab seam sealant on the chains on the other edge so they won't unravel. Allow them to dry, then cut.

5. Tear away the stabilizer one layer at a time.

6. Top-stitch the fringe to your project through the upper row of stitching.

Double fringe

Make a double-sided fringe by wrapping a 2"-wide tripled strip of stabilizer as in preceding steps 1 and 2. Straight-stitch two rows 1/8" apart down the center of the strip. Then follow steps 4 and 5 to complete both sides of the fringe. (Fig. 8-9) Attach the fringe to your project using a satin zigzag stitch, or straight-stitch it on and apply a decorative braid from Chapter 5 over the stitching.

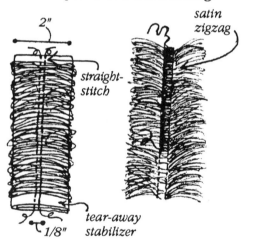

Fig. 8-9: *Stitch down the center of the wrapped chain to make a double fringe.*

Knotted fringe

Knotted fringe is another popular variation. For this technique, the fringe depth should be about 4". Make fringe following the original thread-chain fringe directions. Before applying the fringe, knot bunches of strands together next to the serged edge evenly along the length of the fringe. (Fig. 8-10) Use a crochet hook or loop turner for the easiest knotting. You may need to retrim along the bottom of the fringe to even it before attaching it to your project.

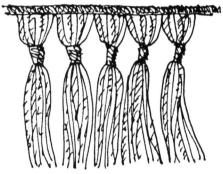

Fig. 8-10: *Evenly knot fringe strands for a novelty trim.*

Project: Fringed Dancing Bag

Don't take the chance of losing your purse at a crowded dance or party. Tuck your few essentials into a pretty little shoulder bag to wear all evening long. (Fig. 8-11)

Foot: Removed for thread chain; standard for fringe and serge-seaming
Stitch: 3-thread
Stitch length: Short for thread chain and fringe; medium for serge-seaming
Stitch width: Wide
Thread: Matching color
 Needle(s): All-purpose or serger
 Upper looper: Pearl rayon or *Decor 6* for thread chain and fringe; all-purpose or serger for serge-seaming
 Lower looper: All-purpose or serger

Fig. 8-11: *Thread-chain fringe decorates this little shoulder bag.*

Tension: Rolled edge for thread chain; balanced for fringe and serge-seaming

Needle: Size 11/75

Fabric: 1/4 yard taffeta for outer bag; 1/4 yard matching lining

Notions: 5" polyester fleece; 5" heavy fusible interfacing; one spool matching ribbon floss for strap; one large snap

1. Cut 5" by 12" rectangles from the taffeta, lining, fleece, and interfacing. Fuse the interfacing to the fleece.

2. From the ribbon floss, make 48" of three-strand thread-chain cording, following the instructions on page 157.

3. Match the ends of the cording to the cut edges of the right side of the lining 2-1/4" from the top on both sides. (Fig. 8-12) With the right sides of the taffeta and lining together, place the fleece on top of the taffeta.

4. Serge-seam the four sides of the bag, leaving an opening at the lower edge for

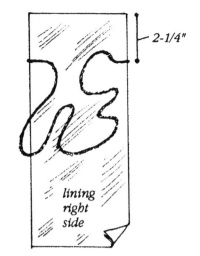

Fig. 8-12: *Position the cording on top of the lining.*

turning and being careful not to catch the cording in the serging. Secure the cording in the seam by straight-stitching again over the cording with a short stitch length.

5. Turn the bag to the right side and fold the opening allowances to the inside. Press carefully. Edge-stitch across the lower edge, closing the opening.

6. At the lower edge, fold 4-1/2" to the wrong side to form the bag. From the right side of the bag, edge-stitch the three unfolded edges. (Fig. 8-13)

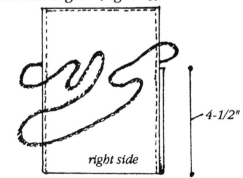

Fig. 8-13: *Fold up the lower edge to form a pocket. Edge-stitch.*

7. Fold the upper edge down at the cording placement, forming the flap. Press lightly.

8. Make a 5" section of 1-1/2"-long fringe, following the previous instructions.

9. Fold under 1/4" on both fringe ends and top-stitch the serge-finished edge onto the lower edge of the flap. (Fig. 8-14) Hand-sew the large snap, securing the flap to the top of the bag.

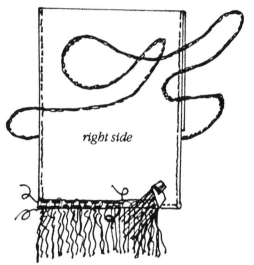

right side

Fig. 8-14: *Top-stitch the fringe to the bag flap, tucking under the ends.*

Lesson 37.
Thread-Chain Tassels

Make tassels from any size of serger thread chain. (Fig. 8-15) For a delicate tassel, use rayon, lingerie, or fine metallic thread. Try pearl cotton, pearl rayon, or crochet thread for a heavier tassel. Rayon thread will make the smoothest chain. Serge at least six yards of chain for one tassel. Smaller chain will require more strands for a fuller appearance.

Fig. 8-15: *Make tassels from any size serger chain.*

1. Loosely wind the chain over a firm piece of cardboard cut to the length of your tassel. The more chain that is wrapped, the fuller the tassel. Do not stretch the chain while winding.

2. Cut a 6" strand of chain for the tassel hanger. Tie the chain together at one end of the cardboard, as shown. (Fig. 8-16) Dab seam sealant on the chains on the opposite end of the cardboard so they won't unravel. Allow them to dry before cutting.

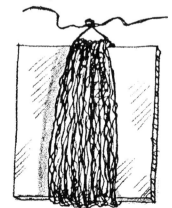

Fig. 8-16: *Tie the chain together at one end of the cardboard.*

3. About 3/4" below the tied end, form a loop of chain and wrap over it. After you have completed the wrapping, thread the chain ends through the loop and pull to secure. (Fig. 8-17) Hide the ends under the edge of the wrapping.

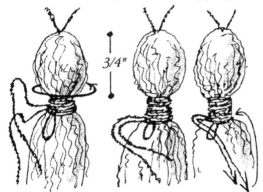

Fig. 8-17: *Form a thread-chain loop and wrap over it. Pull the ends through the loop to secure. Tuck the tails under the wrapping.*

Novelty tassels

■ Make a chunky tassel from the thread-chain cording featured in Lesson 35. Or make tassel thread chain over a heavy filler. (Fig. 8-18)

Fig. 8-18: *Make tassels from cording, too. Quickly wrap any tassel with chain-covered wire.*

■ Cover a 12" length of wire by carefully serging a thread chain over it, using the techniques outlined in Lesson 7. Then use the wire both to tie and wrap the tassel. Thread one wire end under one end of the loops and twist a 1" circle. Hide the twisted wire in the middle of the tassel and twist the loop just above the tassel to secure. (Fig. 8-19) Bring the long end from the center of the tassel and wrap it around diagonally. Feed the end up inside the tassel. Or use the wire to wrap the tassel conventionally.

Fig. 8-19: *Loop one end of the wire and use it to secure the tassel top. Wrap the long end around the tassel and hide the tip inside.*

■ Braid the tassel top. Before wrapping the tassel, hang it from the thread-chain tie. Divide the tassel into three even bunches and braid for about 1-1/2" before wrapping just below the braided area. The depth of the tassel should be about 6" for this option. (Fig. 8-20)

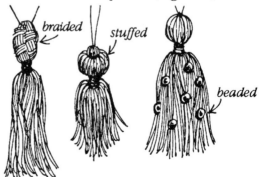

Fig. 8-20: *Possibilities for novelty tassels are practically endless.*

- Stuff the tassel top. Use a ball of matching thread or yarn to fill out the tassel above the wrapping. Then position the threads evenly over the stuffing and wrap conventionally. A fuller tassel is needed to cover the stuffing ball.

- Tie beads, buttons, or other small ornaments onto the tassel tails. Let your imagination be your guide.

Project:
Tassel Napkin Rings

Highlight your table with these glamorous table accessories. A combination of thread-chain cording from Lesson 35 and a serged tassel are all you need. (Fig. 8-21)

Fig. 8-21: Napkin rings show off your serger chain art.

Foot: Removed
Stitch: 3-thread
Stitch length: Short
Stitch width: Any
Thread: Matching color
    Needle: All-purpose or serger
    Upper looper: Decorative thread
    Lower looper: All-purpose or serger
Tension: Rolled edge
Needle: Size 11/75

Notions: 3" by 4-1/2" rectangle of cardboard

1. Serge 14 yards of thread chain for each tassel.

2. Following the directions in Lesson 35 (page 157), make 5-1/2" of cording for each tassel.

3. Center a 5-1/2" cording loop on one short end of the cardboard rectangle with 3/4" ends hanging off the edge. (Fig. 8-22)

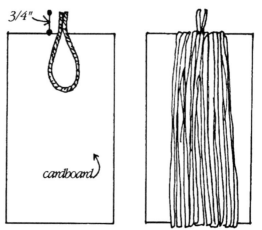

Fig. 8-22: Position the loop on one end of the cardboard and wrap over it loosely, distributing the chain evenly on both sides.

4. Loosely wrap thread chain around the cardboard on both sides of the loop ends. Wrap alternately on both sides, 24 times each.

5. Using a darning needle, thread a 6" strand of thread chain under the loops to tie the top of the tassel. Then stitch

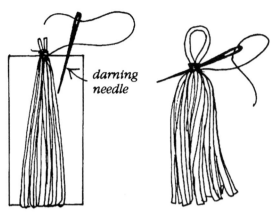

Fig. 8-23: *Tie the top of the tassel and stitch it to the loop ends. After cutting reverse the tassel so the loop is on top. Wrap a few times and tack to secure.*

through the cording loop ends several times to anchor them. (Fig. 8-23)

6. Without unthreading the needle, apply seam sealant to the opposite ends and cut them apart when dry.

7. Turn the tassel right side out with the loop on top. Wrap the needle thread several times around the loop ends just above the tassel. Then make a few small stitches through the wrapping to secure and clip the extra thread (similar to sewing on a button).

8. Using another section of thread chain, wrap the tassel at about 1-1/4" from the top, following the previous instructions.

Lesson 38. Thread-Chain Jewelry

Entire books have been written about creating jewelry, so we can only brush the surface here. Serger thread chain, thread-chain cording, and chain serged over elastic thread all have many jewelry-project applications.

Jewelry findings are available in fabric and craft stores for necklaces and bracelets, earrings, pins, and barrettes. To complement your projects, choose from a wide variety of fashionable beads, available from both stores and mail-order sources.

Circular necklaces and bracelets

Using thread-chain cording or heavy, elastic-filled thread chain, string a large bead to cover a secure knot. (Fig. 8-24)

Fig. 8-24: *Knot the cording and hide it under a large bead.*

Tie the knot until it is large enough to fit snugly inside the bead. String multiple beads on the cording, if desired, before knotting the ends. Use enough cording to slip the bracelet or necklace on and off without untying. Bracelets should be about 8" around, and necklaces must be at least 24" (unless they are made from stretchable cording).

If you'll be wearing several circular necklaces, make them in varying lengths, such as 24", 26", and 28". (Fig. 8-25)

Fig. 8-25: *Wear several circular necklaces or bracelets at once.*

Twisted and hooked necklaces

Several types of hooks and clasps are available. (Fig. 8-26) Choose any type for this easy thread-chain necklace:

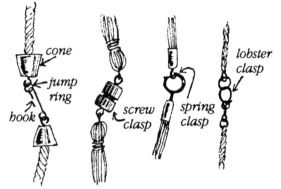

Fig. 8-26: *A variety of closures are available from craft supply sources.*

1. Twist various multiple strands of thread chain or thread-chain cording. The strands should be 1-1/2" longer than the desired necklace length minus the length of the closure.

S **Special Tip:** For a beaded effect on all or part of the necklace strands, serge thread chain over pearls or beads following the guidelines on page 129.

2. Using beading wire or strong thread, wrap the twisted strands together securely, about 3/4" from both ends. (Fig. 8-27)

Fig. 8-27: *Tie the twisted strands together at both ends. Then fold back the ends, wrap, and sew on a closure.*

3. Turn the short ends back over the wrapping and decoratively wrap the ends with matching or coordinating thread chain. Use the wrapping technique for thread-chain tassels explained on page 163.

4. Hand-sew the closure on opposite ends of the necklace.

Shaped thread-chain designs

Serge thread chain over water-soluble stabilizer to help shape it into intricate designs. (Fig. 8-28)

Fig. 8-28: Shape a thread-chain design using a rolled edge serged over water-soluble stabilizer.

Moisten the chain just enough to wash away the visible stabilizer. Some residual stabilizer will remain in the chain. Using a toothpick, shape the chain to dry over waxed paper or aluminum foil. When dry, glue or hand-tack the chain together where it crosses.

Leave ends on the thread-chain design to attach to an earring wire. Or glue a button to an earring backing over the chain ends of the design. (Fig. 8-29)

Fig. 8-29: Make earrings by hanging shaped thread-chain designs from earring findings.

Friendly Plastic

Readily available in craft stores in a wide variety of colors and textures, *Friendly Plastic* is so easy it's practically addictive. Even with your first efforts, you can make attractive jewelry. Form pins, earrings, beads, teardrop ornaments, and even buttons with minimal effort.

Several excellent booklets are available with instructions and project ideas for this interesting medium. Our intention was to combine the plastic with thread chain (or serged stitches on sections of fabric) for another jewelry option.

The more you experiment, the more proficient you'll become. But even the simple projects outlined here look great.

Friendly Plastic softens quickly at a temperature just below boiling. The most popular method for melting the plastic is to dip it into an electric frying pan of water kept constantly at the correct temperature. Use a spatula or tweezers to dip it into the water.

We also found it easy to heat the plastic in a 225- to 250-degree oven on a throwaway aluminum pan. With this method, you can prewrap a section with thread chain before it softens. The plastic cools quickly enough to be handled and manipulated, and it will lift easily off the aluminum surface. And don't worry if the plastic hardens before you've shaped it properly—just reheat it.

Manipulating the plastic with your fingers will leave interesting imprints. If you want a smoother look, work with a plastic sandwich bag over your hand or use a smooth roller.

■ Wrapped pins and earrings

Cut sections of the plastic the size and shape you want for a pin or earrings. Wrap the sections with thread chain and place them face up on the aluminum pan in the preheated oven. If desired, string beads onto the chain before wrapping.

When the plastic has visibly softened (about 1-1/2 minutes), remove it from the oven. Let the plastic cool slightly so you can handle it comfortably, then press the thread chain into the top of the plastic. If desired, squeeze the sides of the plastic to create a raised, irregular shape on top. (Fig. 8-30)

Fig. 8-30: *Wrap thread chain around* Friendly Plastic, *soften it in the oven, and press the chain securely into the plastic before drying.*

As soon as it cools sufficiently, the plastic can be lifted from the pan easily without bending. When the plastic has cooled completely, use epoxy to glue a pin or earring back to the piece.

■ Rolled beads

Cut wedge-shaped pieces of the plastic and roll them around thread-chain cording to make bracelets or necklaces. The larger you cut the wedge, the larger the bead.

When the plastic wedges have softened, press the cording on top of the wide end of the wedge. Then roll the wedge firmly around the cording to form a bead and let it harden. (Fig. 8-31)

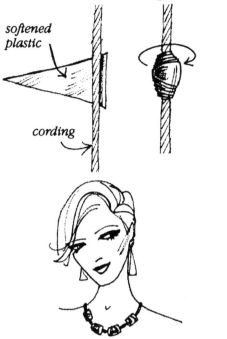

Fig. 8-31: *Wrap a wedge of* Friendly Plastic *securely around the cording to form a bead.*

■ Pendants

Friendly Plastic can be cut both before and after it has been heated. Knot loops of thread chain and press them on top of the heated plastic. Then, while the plastic is still soft, cut around the outside of the loop. (Fig. 8-32)

Use your fingernail or a pointed object (such as a knitting needle) to press designs into one or both sides of the pendant. Using epoxy or clear multipurpose cement, reinforce the bond between the thread chain and the *Friendly Plastic* on each piece. Hang one or more pieces from earring wires or make many pieces and hand-tack them to a strip of elastic for an eye-catching bracelet. (Fig. 8-33)

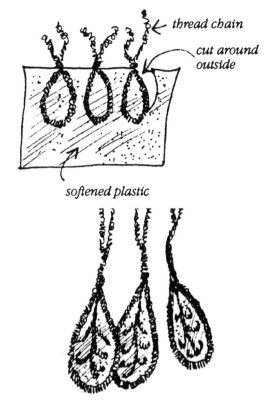

Fig. 8-32: *Make pendants by pressing thread chain onto softened plastic and cutting around the outer edge while it is still soft.*

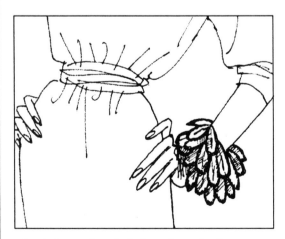

Fig. 8-33: *A lavish fashion bracelet features multiple pendants tacked to an elastic band.*

Project:
Friendly Plastic Pin

Make a fashionable accessory using *Friendly Plastic* and a simple serge-and-heat process. (Fig. 8-34)

Fig. 8-34: *Pin a pleasing display of serger thread chain to your lapel.*

Foot: Removed
Stitch: 3-thread
Stitch length: Short
Stitch width: Any
Thread: Several different colors
    Needle: All-purpose or serger
    Upper looper: Decorative thread
    Lower looper: All-purpose or serger
Tension: Rolled edge (or narrow
    balanced)
Needle: Size 11/75
Notions: 1 small piece of *Friendly
    Plastic;* 1 pin back; epoxy

1. Cut the plastic to about 1-1/2" by 3" if the piece is not already that size.

2. Serge several different colors and textures of thread chain to complement the plastic.

3. Wrap the chain around the plastic randomly to create a pleasing design, and set the piece face-up on an aluminum pan.

4. Put the pan into a preheated 225- to 250-degree oven about 1-1/2 minutes or until the plastic is visibly softened.

5. Remove the pan from the oven. When the plastic is cool enough to touch, press the thread chain into the top of the pin.

6. After cooling, remove the pin from the pan and glue a pin back to the center of the underside, using the epoxy.

Glossary of Serging Terms

All-purpose or serger thread—All-purpose thread usually means cotton-covered polyester wound parallel on conventional spools. Standard serger thread has the same fiber content but is lighter in weight than all-purpose thread and is crosswound on cones or tubes so that it feeds easily during higher-speed serger sewing.

Balanced stitch—A serge-finished edge or seam in which the upper- and lower-looper thread tensions are balanced so the threads meet at the edge of the fabric, forming loops.

Binding—A strip of fabric sewn to an edge, then wrapped around it and secured to hide the seam and the raw edge.

Bite—The distance between the knife and the needle, affecting the amount of fabric in the stitch.

Decorative seam (also decorative exposed seam)—Any seam on the outside of a garment or project that enhances design detail.

Decorative thread (also decorative serging or decorative finish)—Any thread other than all-purpose or serger thread, although even a contrasting color of these threads is technically considered decorative. Our favorite decorative threads include woolly nylon, rayon, pearl cotton, crochet thread, buttonhole twist, and metallic. New threads are introduced regularly.

Ease plus—A manual option to the differential feed, accomplished by force-feeding fabric under the front of the presser foot and holding it from exiting out the back.

Edge-stitch—A medium-length (10-12 stitches/inch) straight-stitch on a conventional sewing machine applied near the edge of anything being sewn. Edge-stitching is often used to join two serge-finished layers.

Filler-cord—Crochet thread, pearl cotton, or buttonhole twist that simulates piping when serged over with a short, satin-length stitch.

Flatlock—A technique by which the needle thread is loose enough so the serged stitches flatten out on top of the fabric, forming decorative loops when the fabric is pulled apart. The underside will show a ladder effect of evenly spaced double parallel stitches. Used for both seaming and decorative stitching on a folded edge, flatlocking lends many creative possibilities.

Heavy thread—Crochet thread, pearl cotton, or buttonhole twist used for serge-gathering or filler-cord in serger piping.

Long stitch—A 4mm or 5mm serged stitch length.

Machine baste—A long (6-8 stitches/inch) straight-stitch on a conventional sewing machine.

Mail order—A growing trend that offers the convenience of at-home catalog shopping. Almost any product is available through mail order, but without the immediate, hands-on selection available at your local fabric store.

Matching thread—Thread the same color as (or that blends as well as possible with) the project fabric.

Medium-length stitch—A serged stitch length of about 3mm.

Medium-width stitch—A serged stitch width of about 3.5mm.

Narrow-width stitch—A 2mm to 3mm serged stitch width. Used to serge a narrow seam or edge.

Ornamental serging (also decorative serging)—Any serger stitching used to artistically enhance a garment or project. Decorative thread, altered tension, or a combination of serging techniques can be used to create ornamental serging.

Ready-to-wear—Garments available for purchase through retail stores and mail-order outlets.

Rolled edge (finish or seam)—Also called a narrow rolled edge or hem, this stitch is created by altering the tension so that the raw edge rolls to the underside. A short stitch length creates an attractive satin-stitch edge.

Satin stitch (satin length)—A stitch length short enough to allow the thread used to cover the entire fabric over which it is serged. Appropriate for both a balanced stitch or a rolled edge.

Serge-finish—Most often a medium-length, medium-width, balanced, 3- or 3/4-thread stitch used to finish the edge of one layer during the construction process.

Serge-gather—Several serger techniques are possible for gathering an edge. You can use the differential feed on the 2.0 setting. Another option is to tighten your needle tension and lengthen your stitch.

Or simply serge over heavy thread with a balanced stitch, being careful not to catch the heavy thread in the serging. Then, after anchoring one end, pull the heavy thread to gather the edge to any specific length. A fourth option is to loosen the needle tension, serge, and then pull up the needle thread.

Serge-seam—Most often a wide, medium-length, balanced, 3- or 3/4-thread stitch used to seam two layers together.

Short stitch—A .75mm to 2mm serged stitch length.

Stitch-in-the-ditch—Stitching directly on top of a previous seamline to secure another layer positioned on the underside. Often used for nearly invisible stitching when applying a binding to an edge.

Straight-stitch—A medium-length (10-12 stitches/inch) straight stitch on a conventional sewing machine.

Thread chain—The joined loops formed by serging on a properly threaded machine with no fabric.

Top-stitch—A conventional-machine straight stitch (10-12 stitches/inch) used to attach one layer (often serge-finished) to another. Top-stitching also can be used as a decorative design detail.

Wide stitch—A 5mm to 9mm serged stitch width.

Woolly nylon—One of our favorite decorative threads that became popular with the advent of serger sewing. A crimped nylon thread, it fluffs out to fill in any see-through spaces on a decorative edge.

Zigzag stitch—A basic stitch on a conventional sewing machine that forms a back-and-forth pattern similar to herringbone.

Mail-Order Resources

We recommend that every serger enthusiast develop a special relationship with his or her local dealers and retailers for convenient advice and inspiration, plus the ease of coordinating purchases. However, when specialty items cannot be found locally, or when a home-sewer lives several miles from a sewing retailer, mail-order specialists are a worthwhile option.

The following list will make your search for mail-order resources a breeze. Our list is for reference only and does not carry our endorsement or guarantee. (We have not knowingly included any questionable items or firms.)

A **Authors' note:** In today's volatile business climate, any mail-order source list will change frequently. Please send your comments on any out-of-business notifications or unsatisfactory service to Tammy Young, 2269 Chestnut #269, San Francisco, CA 94123.

Key to Abbreviations and Symbols:

SASE = Self-addressed, stamped (first-class) envelope

L-SASE = Large SASE (2-oz. first-class postage)

* = refundable with order

= for information, brochure, or catalog

Great Serger Notions

Aardvark Adventures, P.O. Box 2449, Livermore, CA 94551, 415/443-2687. Books, beads, buttons, bangles, plus an unusual assortment of related products. Decorative serging thread, including metallics. $1#.

Clotilde, Inc., 1909 SW First Ave., Ft. Lauderdale, FL 33315, 800/772-2891. Catalog of over 1,200 items, including special serger threads and notions, the *Perfect Pleater* and other sewing tools and supplies, books, and videos. $1#.

The Cutting Edge, P.O. Box 76044, St. Peters, MO 63376. Serger notions, including coned threads (all-purpose and decorative), needle threaders, patterns, and carrying cases. L-SASE#.

Jehlor Fantasy Fabrics, 730 Andover Park West, Seattle, WA 98188, 206/575-8250. Baubles, bangles, and beads. $2.50#.

Kruh Knits, P.O. Box 1587, Avon, CT 06001, 800/248-KNIT. *Rainbow Elastic Plus,* serger threads, and notions. $5#.

Madeira Marketing Ltd., 600 E. 9th St., Michigan City, IN 46360, 219/873-1000. A wide range of their own decorative threads. Free#.

Mill End Store, Box 02098, Portland, OR 97202, 503/236-1234. Broad selection of notions, trims, serger threads, and accessories. SASE#.

Nancy's Notions, Ltd., P.O. Box 683, Beaver Dam, WI 53916, 800/833-0690. Over 300 sewing notions and accessories, serger threads and tools, interfacings and fabrics, books, and videos. Free#.

National Thread & Supply, 695 Red Oak Rd., Stockbridge, GA 30281, 800/847-1001, ext. 1688; in GA, 404/389-9115. Name-brand sewing supplies and notions. Free#.

Newark Dressmaker Supply, P.O. Box 2448, Lehigh Valley, PA 18001, 215/837-7500. Sewing notions, trims, buttons, decorative threads, and serger supplies. Free#.

Sew-Art International, P.O. Box 550, Bountiful, UT 84010. Decorative threads, notions, and accessories. Free#.

Sew/Fit Co., P.O. Box 565, La Grange, IL 60525, 312/579- 3222. Sewing notions and accessories; modular tables for serger/sewing machine setup; books. Free#.

Sewing Emporium, 1087 Third Ave., Chula Vista, CA 92010, 619/420-3490. Hard-to-find sewing notions, sewing machine and serger cabinets and accessories, serger threads, and accessories. $2#.

The Sewing Place, 100 West Rincon Ave., Suite 105, Campbell, CA 95008. Sewing machine and serger needles and feet, plus books by Gale Grigg Hazen. Specify your brand and model when ordering machine accessories. L-SASE#.

The Sewing Workshop, 2010 Balboa St., San Francisco, CA 94121, 415/221-SEWS. Unique designer notions. L-SASE#.

Speed Stitch, 3113-D Broadpoint Dr., Harbor Heights, FL 33983, 800/874-4115. Machine-art kits and supplies, including all-purpose, decorative, and specialty serging threads, books, and accessories. $3*#.

Treadleart, 25834 Narbonne Ave., Suite I, Lomita, CA 90717, 800/327-4222. Books, serging supplies, notions, decorative threads, and creative inspiration. $1.50#.

Worldly Goods, 110 W. Yankie St., Silver City, NM 88061, 505/388-2122. Beads, buttons, and jewelry findings. $4.50#.

YLI Corporation, 482 N. Freedom Blvd., Provo, UT 84601, 800/854-1932 or 801/377-3900. Decorative, specialty, serger, and all-purpose threads, yarns, and ribbons. $1.50#.

Other Books by the Authors

ABCs of Serging, Chilton Book Company, 1991, $16.95. The complete guide to serger sewing basics, by Tammy Young and Lori Bottom.

Distinctive Serger Gifts & Crafts, Chilton Book Company, 1989, $14.95. The first book with one-of-a-kind serger projects using ingenious methods and upscale ideas, by Naomi Baker and Tammy Young.

Innovative Serging, Chilton Book Company, 1989, $14.95. State-of-the-art techniques for overlock sewing, by Gail Brown and Tammy Young.

Innovative Sewing, Chilton Book Company, 1990, $14.95. The newest, best, and fastest sewing techniques, by Gail Brown and Tammy Young.

Know Your baby lock, Chilton Book Company, 1990, $16.95. Ornamental serging techniques for all *baby lock* serger models, by Naomi Baker and Tammy Young.

Know Your White Superlock, Chilton Book Company, 1991, $16.95. Ornamental serging techniques for all *Superlock* serger models, by Naomi Baker and Tammy Young.

Know Your Pfaff Hobbylock, Chilton Book Company, 1991, $17.95. Ornamental serging techniques for all *Hobbylock* serger models, by Naomi Baker and Tammy Young.

Simply Serge Any Fabric, Chilton Book Company, 1990, $14.95. Tips and techniques for successfully serging all types of fabric, by Naomi Baker and Tammy Young.

Taming Decorative Serging, by Tammy Young, 1991, $14.95. A step-by-step workbook teaching special techniques for glamorous decorative serging.

Taming Your First Serger, by Lori Bottom, 1989, $14.95. A hands-on guide to basic serging skills in an easy-to-use workbook format.

Look for these titles in your local stores, or write for a complete, up-to-date listing: Tammy Young, 2269 Chestnut, Suite 269, San Francisco, CA 94123. To order, add $3.50 per book to the listed price for shipping and handling.

Index

About the Authors

Naomi Baker is a nationally recognized serger sewing authority who writes regularly for major industry publications and has co-authored five previous Chilton books with Tammy Young. A home economics graduate of Iowa State University and former extension agent, she worked for Stretch & Sew for ten years. She specializes in technique research and development and is well known for her dressmaking skills.

Naomi has a sewing consulting business and appears across the country at special workshops and conventions. She lives and works in Springfield, Oregon, with her husband and family, huge fabric stash, and an enviable number of sergers and sewing machines.

Tammy Young has combined creativity and practicality in her writing and publishing career. With a home economics degree from Oregon State University, she has an extensive background in the ready-to-wear fashion industry, as well as being a former extension agent and high school home economics teacher. Tammy has co-authored eight previous Chilton books.

Living and working in San Francisco's Marina District, Tammy founded and managed the *Sewing Update* and *Serger Update* newsletters before selling them in 1991. When her hectic schedule allows, she travels stateside and abroad, frequently picking up trends and ideas for her writing.